The New Teacher Book

The New Teacher Book

Finding Purpose, Balance, and Hope
During Your First Years in the Classroom

A RETHINKING SCHOOLS PUBLICATION

THE NEW TEACHER BOOK

Finding Purpose, Balance, and Hope During Your First Years in the Classroom

Edited by Kelley Dawson Salas, Rita Tenorio, Stephanie Walters, and Dale Weiss

RETHINKING SCHOOLS, LTD., is a nonprofit educational publisher of books, booklets, and a quarterly journal on school reform, with a focus on issues of equity and social justice. To request additional copies of this book or a catalog of other publications, or to subscribe to the quarterly journal *Rethinking Schools*, contact:

Rethinking Schools
1001 East Keefe Avenue
Milwaukee, Wisconsin 53212 USA
800-669-4192
www.rethinkingschools.org

The New Teacher Book: Finding Purpose, Balance, and Hope During Your First Years in the Classroom
© 2004, Rethinking Schools, Ltd.

Cover Design: Joanna Dupuis
Page Design: C. C. Krohne
Project Editor: Leon Lynn
Editorial Assistance: Stacie Williams
Layout/Additional Design: Joanna Dupuis
Illustrations: Paul Duquesnoy

Special thanks to the Joyce Foundation for its generous support of this project.

ISBN 0-942961-45-5

This is what we are about:
We plant seeds that one day will grow.
We water seeds already planted, knowing that they hold future promise.
We lay foundations that will need further development.
We provide yeast that produces effects beyond our capabilities.

We cannot do everything
and there is a sense of liberation in realizing that.
This enables us to do something,
and to do it very well.
It may be incomplete, but it is a beginning, a step along the way....

We may never see the end results,
but that is the difference between the master builder and the worker.
We are workers, not master builders,
ministers, not messiahs.
We are prophets of a future not our own.

— *from a poem by Archbishop Oscar Romero*

Contents

CHAPTER THREE
GETTING TO KNOW THE KIDS

CHAPTER FOUR
DEALING WITH THE WORLD BEYOND YOUR CLASSROOM

Acknowledgments

This is the first book any of us has edited. We did not travel this road alone, and we have many people to thank.

Rethinking Schools editors Bill Bigelow, Catherine Capellaro, Linda Christensen, Larry Miller, Stan Karp, Bob Peterson, Kathy Swope, and editorial associates David Levine and Wayne Au helped conceptualize this book, made many fine contributions to it, and continually pushed us to make it clear, concise, and truly useful to new teachers. Mike Trokan and Susan Bates spearheaded the marketing and distribution efforts needed to put this book into teachers' hands. Graphic artists C. C. Krohne and Joanna Dupuis helped bring all the pieces of this book together in a unified package. Editorial assistant Stacie Williams helped us collect those pieces and keep them straight. And Rethinking Schools book editor Leon Lynn shepherded us along the way with patience, nurturance, vision, and much-needed editorial and logistical support.

We also express our sincere thanks to the many new teachers who helped us with this project. At several potluck dinners and evenings of conversation, they shared their stories, questions, ideas, and hopes for the kinds of teachers they want to become. Thanks especially to Imani Banton, Lea Butler, Aron Corbett, Sara Schneider Cruz, Erin Shaffer, Steve Vande Zande, and Floralba Vivas.

We also thank the many talented, dedicated, and idealistic people who continue to enter the teaching profession. It is to you that we dedicate this book.

— *Kelley Dawson Salas*
Rita Tenorio
Stephanie Walters
Dale Weiss

Introduction

Why did you become a teacher?

Some of us chose the teaching profession because we love children, and we want to make a difference in the lives of students, and thus improve the world.

Some of us believe that children need a solid education so they can take their rightful place in society, so they in turn can help society become more just.

And many of us carry fond memories of a special teacher who lit the fire of learning within us, and now we want to pass that light along to the next generation.

Little did we know, as we signed up for those first School of Education classes, that the adventure on which we were about to embark would also be fraught with uncertainty, frustration, hours of internal dialogue, and questions that don't always find easy resolution.

If you're a new teacher and you're supposed to teach tomorrow as you read this, chances are you have at least a couple of butterflies in your stomach.

As fellow teachers, we know the feeling well.

And you may be tempted to toss this book aside and "do what I'm supposed to be doing" instead: grading papers, creating classroom assignments, or figuring out how to deal with a particularly challenging student in homeroom.

We know firsthand how that feels too.

We invite you to put the immediate demands of your classroom on hold for a little while and spend some time with this book, contemplating some of the broader questions of why we teach and how teachers can stay committed to being good teachers during those first hectic years on the job.

It's common for new teachers to question the wisdom of their decision to enter this profession. Many of us find ourselves with little support, minimal time for planning, students who seem to have needs we can't possibly meet, and plummeting school budgets. And it's a fact that the turnover rate is depressingly high among new teachers: 30% quit within their first three years.

But before you despair, flip that statistic around: The majority of new teachers do make it.

We think this book can help you join the ranks of those who stay in teaching. Here you'll find the voices of other teachers — some new to the job, others with wisdom to share that's rooted in decades of classroom time. They offer practical advice for new teachers who know they're committed to kids and the profession, and who have great ideas about where they want to take their teaching, but who need a little help clarifying their vision, translating it to their right-now, day-to-day work in the classroom, and laying a solid foundation to build upon in the years to come.

A Rethinking Schools Vision for New Teachers

But before we go further, we should talk about what we think a successful teacher is. At Rethinking Schools, we subscribe to a definition of "success" that many new teachers don't hear in preservice preparation programs or in their first years on the job.

We are a publishing collective, comprised mostly of active classroom teachers, which has managed to sustain itself for 18 years because we all believe in putting social justice at the heart of our work. We acknowledge the conditions that negatively affect schools and children, including poverty, funding cuts, the pervasive and poisonous effects of racism, and policymakers who aspire publicly to "leave no child behind" yet time and again put up barriers to real reform by pushing shallow schemes that actually hurt schools and children.

We acknowledge these conditions, but we do not throw up our hands in despair and walk away. Instead, we believe that successful teachers must strive, both within their classrooms and in the broader community, to provide a high-quality education for all students.

We believe that successful teachers invite their students' lives, languages, and cultures into the classroom, and that they start building a classroom community on the first day of school. We believe our students need teachers who are skilled in relating to students and families from diverse backgrounds, and who value the richness that diversity brings.

We believe teachers need to provide an academically rigorous curriculum, which prepares students for the challenges that await them outside the classroom. And we believe a central tenet of this academic rigor is teaching students to analyze the world around them, instead of uncritically receiving the messages pushed upon them by the media, the government, and the other powerful forces that shape our world.

We believe teachers must understand that injustice is a reality today, and that children and adults can and should work together to eradicate it.

And we believe that successful teachers dare to care — about students and their lives, about our communities, and about making a difference. Students need teachers who serve as examples, who foster hope that there is always something one can do to bring about a better world. Teachers should teach for social justice.

Setting Realistic Goals for Yourself

We also know that teaching can be a daunting set of challenges for those just starting out. We remember the uncertainty that new teachers face. We know the self-doubt that comes with feeling you have yet to develop the skills and principles needed to pursue your vision of "good teaching."

Remember that in any profession, achieving a vision is a long-term process. We must be patient with ourselves, and avoid the cynicism and despair that affect too many of our colleagues and deprive them of the idealism and determination that first led them to teaching.

By no means are we saying new teachers should "learn how to be a regular teacher first, then start teaching for social justice." Whether your commitment to social activism led you to teaching, or whether your life as a teacher led you to becoming involved in social justice issues, one thing is certain: Both are crucial components of effective teaching. Good teaching and teaching for social justice come from the same place in you. You cannot put the social-justice part of you aside and wait to become a better teacher. You need to do this job from the start with your whole brain, and with all your passion.

This is a lifelong process. The challenge of developing strong curriculum, which you are comfortable with and feel you can adequately carry out, will be with you every day. And as good teachers teach, they also look for ways to reflect on their commitment to children, and ways to reflect on their commitment to living a life in synch with social justice values. If you establish this from the beginning as a regular part of your work as a teacher, then your classroom practice and your work as a social activist will grow to become one integrated whole.

There will still be days when nothing goes the way you want it to in your classroom. Holding on to a vision of the teacher you want to become will help you get through them.

How to Deal with Your New Job

Teaching is so overwhelming because teachers do a million things at once. We move in many circles: with students in our classrooms, with staff in our buildings, and with parents and members of the community beyond the school walls. We work with activists, community groups, and elected officials to try to improve the policies that affect students and public schools. Being a good teacher means learning how to work effectively in each of these worlds, and how to move between them.

Each chapter of this book offers an orientation to one aspect of this work.

Chapter 1, "Getting Off to a Good Start," addresses how to survive the first years, how to start reaching out and building a support network, and how to stay sane and take care of yourself.

Chapter 2, "'What Am I Going to Teach?'" explores some of the options open to new teachers as they create and teach lessons, and offers guidelines for making social justice a focus of your practice from the beginning.

Chapter 3, "Getting to Know the Kids," discusses how to build a strong classroom community, deal with discipline, and otherwise relate to students. We also raise questions about race, class, and language, discuss the importance of these issues, and suggest ways that teachers can directly address them in the classroom. In order to create an equitable environment for our students, we teachers must recognize and unlearn our own biases. This chapter provides a starting point for that long-term process.

Chapter 4, "Dealing with the World Beyond Your Classroom," explores the broader concerns of teaching. Successful teachers must learn to develop professional relationships with colleagues, administrators, and parents, among others. How do we assert our teaching styles, ask for help, or suggest new ideas to colleagues? How do we build relationships with parents: What can we offer them and what can we expect from them? How do we work with administrators, whether they are supportive or critical, effective or ineffective? How can we work in the broader public arena to make schools better? Where else can we turn for information and resources?

Where You Go from Here

Being a good teacher means spending your life teaching, of course, but it also means spending your life thinking about teaching, in a long-term, systemic way. By asking the right questions, by continuously critiquing and improving your practice, and by continuing to examine the work you do in your classroom and how it connects with the larger world, you can achieve your vision and become the teacher you hope to be.

No book can prepare you for all the challenges that your first years as a teacher will hold, and no set of instructions can tell a teacher precisely how to teach for social justice. We hope, however, that this book will raise some questions, provide some encouragement, and offer some advice you'll find useful as you start establishing yourself in your chosen profession.

We hope this is a book you will keep in your backpack, in your desk, or on your nightstand, to read and reflect upon, to dip into now and then when you need a little inspiration.

And we wish you luck taking on the vital, impossible, life-affirming, frustrating, and absolutely essential job we love.

— The Editors

Undivided Attention

A grand piano wrapped in quilted pads by movers,
tied up with canvas straps — like classical music's
birthday gift to the insane —
is gently nudged without its legs
out an eighth-floor window on 62nd Street.

It dangles in April air from the neck of the movers' crane,
Chopin-shiny black lacquer squares
and dirty white crisscross patterns hanging like the second-to-last
note of a concerto played on the edge of the seat,
the edge of tears, the edge of eight stories up going over, and
I'm trying to teach math in the building across the street.

Who can teach when there are such lessons to be learned?
All the greatest common factors are delivered by
long-necked cranes and flatbed trucks
or come through everything, even air.
Like snow.

See, snow falls for the first time every year, and every year
my students rush to the window
as if snow were more interesting than math,
which, of course, it is.

So please.

Let me teach like a Steinway,
spinning slowly in April air,
so almost-falling, so hinderingly
dangling from the neck of the movers' crane.
So on the edge of losing everything.

Let me teach like the first snow, falling.

— *Taylor Mali*

CHAPTER ONE

Getting Off to a Good Start

Time to Learn

My alarm had not yet gone off, but I was wide awake. My stomach was in knots and I knew I would not be able to eat breakfast. I longed to turn over, go back to sleep, wait for the alarm, hit snooze.

But there was no way. It was September, a school day, a few weeks into my first year of teaching.

I was teaching third grade at a bilingual school on Milwaukee's south side. Those who had hired me and placed me in a fast-track alternative teacher certification program had been eager to get me into the classroom. But on mornings like this, I felt I'd been misled, that I'd been tricked into taking this job without enough training, and with no real idea of what to expect. I was spending six hours a day in my classroom and nearly another six hours planning, rehearsing, and worrying. Even sleep became an extension of my job, as I searched my dreams for the perfect combination of compassion, creativity, and classroom control.

BY
KELLEY
DAWSON
SALAS

Needless to say, I hadn't found the magic formula, either in my classroom or in my dreams. I worried that my teaching career was going to be short-lived.

I dragged myself out of bed and called a

friend. My worries poured forth: I'm no good at this. It's too hard for me to learn the things I need to learn. There are so many jobs that would be easier and pay better. Finally, I called the question: Should I just walk away from this whole thing?

My friend's advice proved wise. The job of a first-year teacher is hard enough, he said. Don't add to your difficulties by beating up on yourself. Let up a little so you have the time and the space to become a good teacher.

I took the advice. I stopped thinking I would conquer the teaching profession in my first few months on the job. Yet my fears persisted. The kind of teacher I wanted to become was fairly clear in my mind. But it seemed to have nothing to do with the reality I experienced every day. I wondered how I could ever get there.

Ideals vs. Reality

I knew I wanted to build a classroom community in which students felt safe, both emotionally and physically. I wanted each student to be able to bring his or her cultural background and experiences into the classroom and to feel important and valued. I hoped to create an atmosphere of respect and cooperation. I wanted students to "behave themselves" without feeling threatened or burdened by punishments. I was also committed to high academic expectations and helping each student learn and progress. I wanted to infuse an anti-racist, social justice perspective into my classroom and I hoped to share my own background as a political activist with my students. I wanted to encourage my students to think critically and to learn to take action to create a more just world.

I was teaching in a two-way bilingual classroom, where both English-dominant and Spanish-dominant students came together and instruction took place in both languages. I knew it was going to be a challenge to meet my students' diverse cultural and academic needs, especially in reading and language proficiency. I also knew that as an Anglo teacher in a classroom of Latino and African-American students, I would have to examine my actions and interactions through a critical lens. I would have to listen to parents and to other teachers, especially parents and teachers of color.

Those were the ideals and beliefs that had led me to become a teacher. Once I actually started teaching, however, reality soon set in. I struggled with discipline, organization, and curriculum. I felt disil-

lusioned when my students seemed more comfortable with an author-
itarian style rather than one which emphasized self-discipline. I found
little support for teaching about
social justice and anti-racism.
Administrators, colleagues, and
classmates in my certification program were willing to listen to my
ideas, but they did not respond as
enthusiastically as I had hoped. No
one seemed eager to collaborate,
or to offer ideas to help me
improve my teaching.

Faced with trying to do and
learn everything at the same time,
I sought advice from as many people as I could. I heard different
messages and it was hard to know
whom to listen to. For example,
some educators told me that I
needed to use borderline-authori-
tarian classroom management
techniques. Once I was "experienced," they said, I could vary
them. My teaching style reflected
my ambivalence about that advice.
Some days, I tried to understand
why certain students were misbe-
having. I talked with students,
showed compassion, called home,
held conferences. But at other
times I became tired of this and
allowed myself to follow a veteran
teacher's well-intentioned but flawed advice: "With this group, you'll
just have to act like a drill sergeant."

> **VOICES**
> **FROM THE**
> **CLASSROOM**
>
> "IT'S USEFUL FOR NEW
> teachers to reflect on the
> difference between being a
> 'good person' and being a
> 'good teacher.' It is impor-
> tant to be nurturing and
> supportive of your students,
> but it's also important to
> challenge them to work hard
> and to help them assume
> responsibility for making
> their own schooling success-
> ful. If you're able to main-
> tain a little critical distance
> to reflect on situations and
> not internalize or personal-
> ize everything, it will help
> smooth out the emotional
> ups and downs, which can
> get pretty intense."
>
> — Stan Karp

I felt that part of the discipline puzzle would be solved if I could
just offer my students good, engaging lessons. And yet I was overwhelmed by the task of choosing the content I wanted to teach. Again,
the advice I received and expectations laid out for me were traditional:
Follow the curriculum. I was sent to inservices on the basal, a pro-

gram called Power Writing, and our district's new math series. I could see some value in each, but I also saw gaping holes. The social studies curriculum, in particular, seemed worlds away from what I wanted to teach. The textbook was almost impenetrable and seemed totally disconnected from the lives of my students. But I was using it because I wasn't sure what else to do.

The assessment program was equally circumscribed. Our district requires lots of standardized testing and test preparation. School administrators handed me a stack of Target Teach materials in October and told me to administer four practice reading tests before the actual reading test in March. They expected me to tabulate the results of each practice test and re-teach the specific testing skills that my students lacked.

Subtle Steps Forward

I spent the fall sorting through the various expectations and figuring out where and how they related to my own goals. As first semester ended, I had made little progress in teaching social justice issues. But I had experimented with creating a positive classroom community and an organized, disciplined environment. I had also begun to pick and choose useful pieces from my school's reading, writing, and math curricula.

One example was my evolving reading program. Like many teachers, I had little access to multiple copies of books outside of our basals. In the beginning of the year, I followed the advice of administrators and my mentor in my certification program: I used my teacher's guide faithfully and trudged through the basal story by story. But by mid-semester I scrapped this plan and was picking selected stories. I also dropped many of the suggested lessons and invented my own. Instead of dutifully teaching "The Three Little Hawaiian Pigs," which felt like a superficial attempt to put a multicultural spin on a traditional tale, I chose to teach more true-to-life stories such as *Halmoni and the Picnic,* a children's book by Sook-Nyul Choi about a Korean immigrant girl and her grandmother, and *Chicken Sunday,* Patricia Polacco's story built around intergenerational, cross-cultural friendships. I helped students compare the cultural backgrounds of the characters in *Chicken Sunday,* and discussed why Halmoni might feel shy about having her classmates meet her grandmother.

It was not exactly where I wanted to be, but it was a subtle step in the right direction.

In January I decided to take a further step away from the "traditional" follow-the-book advice offered to new teachers: I didn't want to wait to teach about issues of racism and social justice. Perhaps this was the first time that I felt I had enough of the basics in place to spend significant time working on my own curriculum. Or perhaps I realized that the time would never be "just right."

Justice and Civil Rights

In preparation for our school's African-American history program in February, I taught a unit on the Civil Rights Movement, drawing ideas from a *Rethinking Schools* article by Kate Lyman. As we began I was floored to learn that my third graders had very little understanding of the concept of "rights." Our studies centered around the Montgomery, Alabama, bus boycott and the integration of the schools in Little Rock, Arkansas. We discussed racism, discrimination, justice, rights, mass movements, and freedom. Students wrote and performed a play about the bus boycott. They researched famous people of color who had fought for change. For the first time, I felt I was attempting the kind of teaching I wanted to do.

I was also acutely aware of my unit's limitations. It focused on the changes brought about by the Civil Rights Movement, but downplayed the racism and injustice that continue today. Our studies highlighted the achievements of a few well-known leaders, but somewhat underplayed the important contributions made by thousands of other participants. And despite my fledgling awareness of different theories of multicultural/anti-racist education, I did not manage to include activities that helped students themselves become activists in identifying and fighting the racism that existed in their own community.

Despite these weaknesses, I learned a lot teaching that unit. One important lesson: Teaching about something real and important is more effective in creating an orderly, disciplined classroom environment than acting like a drill sergeant.

Just as I was beginning this unit, my mentor said she wanted me to work on discipline. She insisted that I needed to be firmer and more consistent with my students. "You aren't going to like doing it," she told me, "but you have to do it."

I agreed with my mentor that my discipline had been inconsistent. But I felt this was partly because I had not been teaching the quality of lessons my students deserved. During the Civil Rights Movement unit, I was able to offer lessons that I believed were worth their time. I also felt fewer qualms about consistently applying our classroom rules; rule enforcement stopped being a series of punishments for bored students and instead became a prerequisite to accomplishing serious and relevant learning.

Standardized Tests

The moment was sweet, but it didn't last long. By March, the third grade reading test was upon us. My teaching was derailed for three weeks as I coaxed, prodded, and bribed my students through their first experience with a standardized test. Going into the testing, I thought my students were well-prepared. But nonetheless the testing process was grueling.

I felt very official as I followed my test administrator's script: "You may now begin the test." Immediately, two students began to cry.

Q/A

What are some ways I can start building a support system for myself?

It's vital to establish numerous support networks. These will give you ideas and shoulders to cry on, keep you creative, and in the long run, will keep you in the profession.

Some people choose to establish peer-to-peer critique groups. Others find support by establishing curriculum groups in their discipline or study groups to read and discuss books of interest. You might consider meeting with a few friends or colleagues to discuss articles in the journal *Rethinking Schools*.

Start modestly. Combine socializing and support. One teachers' group I know holds sessions they call "Sunday Night at the Movies." They get together to watch videos that they might want to use in their classrooms. They begin with snacks, watch the video, and then critically evaluate the video and brainstorm possible classroom uses. Non-teaching spouses are invited so that this doesn't feel overly like a "work" meeting.

— Bill Bigelow

I made a beeline for one of them and our teaching assistant headed for the other. After 15 minutes of sweet-talking, trips to the drinking fountain, and pats on the back, all of the students were working on the test.

I walked around, looking over students' shoulders and trying to maintain a positive outward appearance. Inside, I worried. I was not overly concerned about how students would do on the test, but wondered how this stressful experience would affect the confidence of several students who didn't have a lot of self-esteem to lose. Even though I prefaced the test-taking with weeks of "this doesn't really tell people anything about who you are," some students felt great pressure to succeed.

VOICES FROM THE CLASSROOM

"BEING A TEACHER IS NOT an occupation that exists within you only when you are on location. Being a teacher permeates every fiber of your being all of the time. It is something that never leaves you."

— Kathy Swope

(I didn't receive the results of the reading test until almost the last week of school. The principal presented them to my partner teacher and me with a comment of congratulations — our students had done well. I fought the urge to be proud, forcing myself to remember that the test was not a particularly accurate or useful measure of students' reading skills (or of my teaching skills). I smiled, thanked my principal, filed the result sheet away, and went on with my day. My students and I had gone through a lot and the final chapter felt anticlimactic.)

There was no let-up after the third grade reading test. Evenings and weekends, I still struggled to find the energy to attend classes and complete my certification program. Before I knew it, I was staying up late to finish my last round of report cards. I had made it through my first year.

Lessons from My First Year

What did I accomplish during that whirlwind of a first year? Looking back, I can see that my uncertainty at the beginning of the year and the conservative advice I received made for a slow start. It took time to pull together a group of people whose advice I accepted and trusted, to sort through the demands of my school and district, and to feel confident enough to assert my own vision. It took some experimenting to see that discipline is not a question of bossing students but of providing interesting, challenging material and helping them meet the challenge.

It seems ironic to me now that I spent so much time fretting over such things. I know I have to provide an organized, disciplined classroom environment, and administer state-mandated standardized tests. But I do not have to act like a boss, follow a prescribed "teacher-proof" curriculum, or agree to excessive test-prep activities. As a professional I have the authority to do what I think is most beneficial to my students.

During that first year I caught glimpses of myself doing the kind of teaching I wanted, but it wasn't much to show for a whole year. I reminded myself of the advice that had served me well all year: Don't get too down on yourself; maintain high expectations but take time and space to develop your skills.

I learned that it was easy to become isolated in my classroom and that it takes extra energy to connect with other educators. Equally important, I learned that without such outside help, it's difficult to grow.

Part of the confidence I needed to take even small steps in advancing my vision came from conversations with colleagues. Although I continued to feel overwhelmed by the traditional nature of my professional training, I pulled together a loose cadre of teacher friends and co-workers and talked with them regularly. In particular, teacher friends that I had long known through political activism offered encouragement and support.

Pulling together a supportive group of colleagues during one's first year of teaching can seem like just one more burden, but I found it worth the extra effort. There was no one place where I found support.

As part of my alternative certification, I attended class twice a week with new teachers going through the same experience I was. I collaborated with colleagues at school. I attended events held by education activist groups such as Rethinking Schools. It has made a difference.

I often still feel the way I did on that September morning during my first month of teaching: dissatisfied and worried that I am not making enough progress. While keeping a critical eye on my own practice, I have also begun to think more critically about teacher education programs. Even though I am now certified, I still need ongoing professional training. Like many new and veteran teachers, I need help with effective teaching methods, curriculum, classroom organization, and discipline. Like all teachers, I need help examining my biases, developing culturally competent practices, and being a teacher that works against racism and classism in our schools instead of reinforcing them.

I often feel that these responsibilities fall squarely on my own shoulders and that there is little support from the educational system. This, I think, is what leads so many new teachers to drop out.

Whenever I feel overwhelmed by the lack of support, I fight the urge to leave teaching. Instead, I try to speak up about what teachers need to succeed.

As I struggle toward my vision of good teaching, I remind myself of what I have accomplished so far. I am less isolated and have close ties with other progressive teachers. I am more confident about developing curriculum and a teaching style that reflect my politics. I still need time and guidance, but some of the conditions are in place for me to someday become the teacher I want to be.

I have a long way to go. But I'm on my way. ■

References

Chicken Sunday, by Patricia Polacco (New York: Puffin, 1998).
Halmoni and the Picnic, by Sook-Nyul Choi (Boston: Houghton Mifflin, 1993).
"From Snarling Dogs to Bloody Sunday," by Kate Lyman, in *Rethinking Schools,* Vol. 14, No. 1, Fall 1999. Available online at www.rethinkingschools.org/newteacher.

Where We Might Begin With Teaching

Charles Dickens published *Hard Times* in London in 1854. I'll do the math for you — that's 150 years ago. In the opening paragraphs Dickens transports his readers into the fraught world of a 19th century English classroom, and describes with fierce precision the first thing future teachers need to know:

> Now, what I want is, Facts. Teach these boys and girls nothing but Facts. Facts alone are wanted in life. Plant nothing else, and root out everything else. You can only form the minds of reasoning animals upon Facts: nothing else will ever be of any service to them. This is the principle on which I bring up my own children, and this is the principle on which I bring up these children. Stick to Facts, Sir!"...
>
> The speaker, and the schoolmaster ... swept with their eyes the inclined plane of little vessels then and there arranged in order, ready to have imperial gallons of facts poured into them until they were full to the brim.

The speaker is Thomas Gradgrind, proprietor of a school; the newly hired schoolmaster is the famously named Mr. M'Choakumchild, recently graduated from a teachers college, or as Dickens would have it, "turned" with 140 colleagues "at the same time, in

BY
WILLIAM
AYERS

the same factory, on the same principles, like so many pianoforte legs.... He had been put through an immense variety of paces, and had answered volumes of head-breaking questions. Orthography, etymology, syntax, and prosody, biography, astronomy, geography...." The list climbs higher, intermittently earnest and ridiculous, and ends with Dickens' quick commentary: "Ah, rather overdone, M'Choakumchild. If he had only learnt a little less, how infinitely better he might have taught much more."

This is where most teachers in Victorian England were expected to begin. Each was expected to be found front and center behind a lectern or a desk, holding sway with an iron hand, dispensing bits of curriculum with an august authority. Each was to think of himself as lord and commander of all he surveyed, the master of his little ship.

In 21st-century America the metaphor of master and commander seems all the more entrenched. This is where we're expected to begin. We might, however, search for more honest and more hopeful images. We might, for example, acknowledge from the start that we are, each of us, at whatever age or state of life or career, free people who are still learning, still curious, still searching. We are, then, neither masters nor slaves, but, rather, pilgrims. We lose perhaps a sense of stability and finiteness in this image, but we gain a more honest appraisal of the adventure of teaching. We might know a little less, and paradoxically we might then teach much more.

This is where we might begin: Let's not let our lives make a mockery of our values. We want to live consciously and purposefully, as aware as we can be, as engaged and connected as we can become, as energetic and active and present to life's demands and potential as possible. Let's embrace all the loveliness of the world and oppose all the unnecessary suffering and injustice we can see, all the pain human beings are forced to face. The revolutionary leader Rosa Luxemburg captured this feeling in a letter to a friend from her German prison cell in 1917: "Then see to it you remain a Mensch!" she wrote. "Being a Mensch means happily throwing one's life on 'fate's great scale' if necessary, but, at the same time, enjoying every bright day and every beautiful cloud...." So let's aspire to be Mensches.

> **"Mensch"**
> A Yiddish term meaning a person who is honorable, responsible, and strong of character.

Each of us, of course — each of you, each of your students — is born into a "going world," a dynamic site of action and interaction stretching back into deep history and forward toward infinity. Each of us encounters an historical flow, a social surround, a cultural web. And each of us — each of you, each of your students — faces the task of developing an identity within the turmoil of multiplicity, of inventing and reinventing a self in a complex tangle of relationships and conflicting realities, of finding an "I" against a hard backdrop of facticity and "thingification."

Romantic hopes and idealistic dreams, however, always contend with cold reality, with the hard edges and facts of life. None of us is born free; each of us, rather, is thrust into a world not of our choosing. We invent ourselves, then, within a resistant world, holding it, interacting with it, fighting it, changing it. We are both fated and free, free and fated — neither entirely scripted and entangled, nor exactly limitless. We are on a voyage through life, incomplete, moving, changing both the world and ourselves.

> **VOICES**
> **FROM THE**
> **CLASSROOM**
>
> "GOOD TEACHERS DEVELOP over time as they create successful curriculum and learn their craft. But your core values remain a guide to keep you on course, and they'll make themselves felt in endless ways in your classroom."
>
> — Stan Karp

◆ ◆ ◆

For new teachers the hard realities of schooling can come as a slap in the face: too many kids and too little time — the structuring of predictable failure — not enough support and inadequate resources, a sense of terminal isolation. School routines, program expectations, packaged curriculum, and administrative demands bump up against the illusion of just a few months ago: "When I have my own classroom, I'll be free to teach exactly as I want to." Well, it turns out not to be so.

It's easy in these circumstances to condemn your "youthful idealism," to ah-hem about "the real world," and to begin the deadly retreat into cynicism and despair. Too many schools, after all, reward obedience and conformity (in students, and no less in their teachers) while punishing initiative and courage; too many schools wall teachers off from one another and the chance of any meaningful collaboration while creating a culture of complaint, constructing a norm of whining to one another about the kids, their mothers, the community. Where once we were lively, tumultuous idealists, clamoring for authenticity and noisily disillusioned with the world we inherited — a hypocritical, cruel, compromised, and false world — we find ourselves suddenly ready to grow up, almost eager to accede.

There's much in the school, of course, that you can't immediately get right — although you can get together with colleagues, kids, and parents to figure out effective ways to work for some hopeful change. There's also much that you can resist, and always much more that you can control if you pay close enough attention. One of my happiest acts of resistance occurred when I was teaching in New York City: The intercom had interrupted my class countless times on that first morning, and so when the kids were at lunch, I cut the wires, and then dutifully reported to the office a non-working PA. It took them five years to get around to repairing it.

There's an alternative to acceding completely or whining constantly, and it begins with thinking through and naming the commitments you bring with you into the classroom, your values, your pledge. These are not pure abstractions, but rather standards to hold in mind. A fundamental commitment might involve taking the side of your students, affirming the humanity of each and resisting anything that constrains or reduces them. Another might be to create in your classroom an environment that is a kind of republic of many voices, allowing every student a space to be seen and heard and known well as a person of worth and value.

Because teachers work in a fluid, complex, idiosyncratic world, and because there's much beyond our immediate control, it makes sense to focus on these things that you can control. First, you can see your students as whole human beings, three-dimensional beings much like yourself with hopes and dreams, bodies and minds and spirits. You can see with your own eyes, your own curious and critical mind, your own generous heart. And you can resist the alphabet soup of deficits and the toxic habit of labeling kids that infects most schools. No one can make you see kids as creatures with labels clinging to them like barnacles, sharp and ugly. You have a mind of your own, and you can become a student of your students in spite of everything. This gesture alone can be full of surprise, and deeply satisfying. Second, you have more control over the environment for learning than you might think. No one will prevent you from bringing a plant into your classroom; no one will stop you from putting maps on the walls or books on the shelves. What do you want the environment to do and to say?

In a lovely French documentary called "To Have and To Be" Georges Lopez, a middle-aged, one-room schoolhouse teacher in rural France, cares for a dozen or so youngsters who appear to range in age from 5 or 6 to about 12. The film opens with a long, still shot of the empty classroom — chairs on desks, brightly painted pictures everywhere, plants, photographs, pencils, and markers. It is the classroom at rest, and one anticipates a sudden explosion of youthful energy as the day begins. But the camera lingers. And then, without fanfare, a turtle steps from beneath a bookshelf, and then another. We watch the two plod slowly across the floor in a ponderous point, counterpoint.

The dance of the turtles is a metaphor for Lopez's teaching: Everything is slow, nothing hurried. In a world of instant everything, of moving sidewalks and staircases, of fast food and processed words, Lopez acknowledges that the growth of a human being takes time. There is time to get deeply involved, time to pursue projects, time to make and correct mistakes, and time to resolve the little conflicts that will always erupt in a group. There is a purposeful but human rhythm to the day. There is little evidence of the characteristic superficial encounter and the hurried plan — minutes here, minutes there — the curriculum of "I know; you don't know." All five senses are engaged, big kids helping littler ones, everyone with responsibilities, expectations, jobs, goals, and limits. There's a palpable feel of growth and change, an exhilaration that our classroom now is not as it was yesterday, or as it will be tomorrow, and neither are the students or the teacher. They are on a voyage with no clear beginning and no end in sight. While everyone in the classroom helps to shape its contours, it's clear that Lopez's intelligence, values, and priorities are worked up in this space. He is the architect of this space.

In a public second-grade classroom in Chicago I could feel the expression of another distinct intelligence, another classroom architect at work. I saw a job chart, a clean-up chart, a free-time chart, and a chart of favorite books; a street map, a transit map, and several distinctly different world maps sharing space with student-made maps of the classroom, the neighborhood, and their own homes; a cooking area with a "juice bar" and colorful posters depicting "Noodles," "Chile," "Mushrooms," "Cheeses of the World," and "Natural Dyes"; each child's specific self-authored and hand-made stamp, diary, dictionary, thesaurus, "tiny books," icon, math books, puzzles, and board games; puppets; blocks; a bowl of leaves; a sofa and a rug; two large tree stumps; and a bin of scrap wood. The teacher's intentions, purposes, intelligence, and values were on display.

◆ ◆ ◆

Charles Dickens introduces his fictional schoolmaster M'Choakumchild in a chapter called "Murdering the Innocents," a brief meditation on the dangers of imagination and choice, free will and fancy to the men of facts, the people in power. Dickens offers us a glimpse into the coercion, humiliation, and degradation that characterize the classroom as slave galley, where the teacher's task is simply to beat the drum. The chapter ends with Dickens turning to and addressing the schoolmaster directly: "Say, M'Choakumchild. When ... thou shalt fill each jar brim full by-and-by, dost thou think that thou wilt always kill outright the robber Fancy lurking within — or sometimes only maim him and distort him!"

Humanistic teachers need to develop an entirely different rhythm, sometimes in the cracks and crevices of the classrooms we are given. We begin with a many-eyed approach: an eye on your students and an eye on yourself, an eye on the environment for learning and an eye on the contexts within which your work is embedded. You need an eye on reality and another on possibility.

You might end each day asking, "What didn't I do well today? Could I have done better with this student or that one? What alternatives exist?" And you might start the next day forgiving yourself for your lapses and shortcomings, ready to start again. Without self-criticism, teachers can become too easily satisfied, and then self-righteous. But without acceptance they are vulnerable to self-loathing, to berating themselves unnecessarily. Criticism and forgiveness — this is the path to wisdom in teaching. We are, each one of us, a work-in-progress. We are pilgrims who see our students as unruly sparks of meaning-making energy on a voyage through their lives. We, too, are on a journey: Let's create a teaching life worthy of our teaching values. ■

Getting Your Classroom Together

S ometimes the top of my desk at school looks worse than the floor of my teenage daughter's bedroom, which is quite an accomplishment, really. But despite the appearance of disorganization on the top layer of my desk, my years of teaching have taught me lots of ways to better organize my classroom. Perhaps the following thoughts will help.

Paying Attention to the Basics

From the start get ideas from other teachers and consult with them on a wide range of issues. Veteran teachers appreciate being asked for advice. Use only what you think is worthwhile. Take the time to visit as many classrooms as you can and get ideas about everything from wall displays to seating arrangements.

Keep in mind that how you organize your classroom is a reflection on what you think about your students and how you view teaching. For example displaying students' work on the wall can serve as an affirmation of the importance of student voice in your classroom, but depending on what and how such work is chosen it might also privilege certain groups of students and disadvantage others. (For example, if only the "best" work is always displayed, certain students

BY
BOB
PETERSON

26

will rarely have a chance to have their work displayed.)

Similarly a "theater-style" seating arrangement engenders a more lecture-based, teacher-centered approach to teaching, versus other seating arrangements. Sometimes these things which appear to be invisible are part of a "hidden curriculum" and carry powerful messages to students.

The central questions you should ask when organizing your classroom are "Why am I doing this this way?" and "What purpose will it serve?" For example, in some classrooms it's important that students have access to certain materials, books, or calculators. If that's the case, what's the easiest way these things can be made accessible, yet kept orderly and safe? Similarly, classrooms have bulletin boards. Ask yourself, "Why do I have this display up? What purpose does it serve?

Labeling

I am a great believer in labeling. I label plastic dish pans to categorize different genres and levels of student books; I label boxes and drawers and box shelves so that students not only know where things are, but also where they should be returned. A computer, a printer, and some clear contact paper work wonders when it comes to making neat-looking signs to keep things in order.

Seating Arrangements

The students' seating arrangement is crucial to a successful classroom and reflects how the teacher wants to run the class. I vary my seating arrangements depending on the nature of the particular group of kids, the number of students in my classroom, and my current goals for the class.

For me flexibility is key, because at different times I want students to be facing the overhead projector observing a lesson, facing another student in partners, facing a small group, or facing the whole class for a class discussion or class meeting. Obviously no one seating pattern satisfies all those needs. Many elementary teachers arrange their class so that there's a carpet or meeting area where all student can gather in a circle or group for conversation. Some teachers put desks in groups of four or six for the benefit of having "base" groups in their classroom to help with cooperative group activities and classroom management (for a more detailed discussion, see "The Challenge of Classroom Discipline" on page 174).

Modeling

Regardless of the seating arrangement I may be using at a certain time, I model for my students how we get into other arrangements. For paring they must sit "eye-to-eye" and "knee-to-knee." For small groups they have to be facing the center point of their table or desks. For classroom meetings, they need to learn how to pick up their desks and chairs and rearrange them in a safe and quiet manner. I model a lot at the beginning of the year, showing students exactly how each of these maneuvers should be performed. I also find it necessary to occasionally model them again throughout the entire school year.

Displaying Materials

The display of educational materials is also central to a successful classroom. I have a book corner, a writing center with various types of paper and story starters, a geography area, an art supply drawer, a dictionary and resource center, computers, and a math manipulative cart. I have a specific space for "the poster of the week" and a special display area for the daily agenda, announcements, and the song of the week.

One way I vastly expand the space that I have for displaying word lists, posters, etc. is by stringing a strong cord at a height of about eight feet between two perpendicular walls in the front corner of the classroom. Using store-bought skirt hangers (the kind with two move-

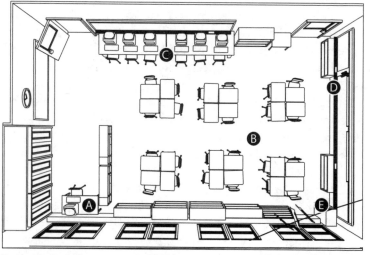

A. Teacher's desk   **B.** Students' desks   **C.** Computer stations
D. Clothespin chart (see page 181 for details)   **E.** Display hangers

able clamps), I can easily hang 12" x 18" tag board sheets, upon which I list words, math solving strategies, etc.

Wall displays are always contradictory: Teachers need to strike a balance between displaying student work and putting up challenging questions, posters, maps, and displays. As you strive to strike a balance, remember that care should be taken to ensure that the students "see themselves on the walls," both literally — the walls of have pictures of students and their work — and figuratively, so the people students see in posters reflect the nationalities of the classroom and the broader world.

Another way to help students see themselves on the walls: At the beginning of the year, on part of my bulletin board I place a large map of our city, marked with a large sign that says, "Where We Live." I have each student place a labeled stick pin in the map to show exactly where they live, and I display essays about the students' neighborhoods nearby.

Organizing the Paper Load

A key part of classroom organization is managing the paperwork — whether it's the school fliers that are to be passed out to the students or homework and class projects that need to be assessed and returned.

Think through a filing system that will grow with you throughout the year, perhaps divided by subject area, unit, or class. If you want to deal with the growing piles of papers on your desk, remember to "handle a piece of paper only once" as a way to save time and better organize your materials. This requires a filing system that is broad enough to include all aspects of school life and flexible enough to allow for new issues.

Talk with other teachers about how they organize their own crush of papers and how they give helpful and timely feedback to students' work. It's no easy task. I have found that occasionally I spend significant time commenting on students' work, but then don't plan sufficient time for students to read and actually learn from my comments.

Communication

Clear communication with students and parents is an essential part of classroom organization. Remember that not all students are auditory, and in particular students learning English as a second language have special learning needs. Explain things in writing as well as orally, through frequent use of the chalkboard, overhead projector, or hand-outs. I write down the daily agenda, homework assignments (which students must copy), and announcements so everyone is aware both auditorily and visually.

Organizing Student Materials

Another crucial part of an organized classroom is helping students learn how to be organized. This is an ongoing task throughout the

What should I be thinking about when I am setting up my classroom?

You and your students will be sharing this space for many months. There is a long-term benefit to working toward making your students feel safe and comfortable in the classroom. And helping them learn to take ownership of their space is an important part of building the classroom community.

Take time over the first weeks to introduce students to the procedures and processes that they will need to know to make the room a positive environment for everyone. Even the youngest children can learn to take responsibility for the materials, rules, and activities that take place there.

Make the environment as organized and child-centered as possible. Make sure there is a space for each child to store materials. Label and store games and materials in ways that make it easy for students to take them out and put them back. Recognize that the set-up you use during the first weeks might need to change as you get to know your students and how they work.

Consider the kinds of tasks you will be asking your students to do. Is there a space for whole-group activities? Are there spaces where kids can work in partners or small groups? Are the materials students will need kept in places they can reach?

Bulletin boards and display space can be a collaborative effort with your students. Be sure that the images displayed in your classroom reflect the students and their families. If there is career of a student. I start by giving each of my fifth graders a "peoples' textbook," a three-ring binder with dividers to organize and maintain non-textbook materials. I learned this approach from a high school social studies teacher who gave his students many supplemental materials but was frustrated by their inability to hold on to them. I explicitly dictate the divider categories — songs, poems, words, history, news, science, and math — and make clear where each handout should be placed. In addition to dividers I give students formatted sheets for writing down what goes in some sections — such as the song or poetry section where students list the singer and song, or poet and title of poem. At the end the year the students are allowed to keep these binders and most do.

Tracking Student Progress

Part of classroom management is not only the grading and managing of papers and other forms of student work, but keeping all that assess-

---

not a lot of diversity in your group, be sure to include pictures, books, and other materials that show a variety of colors and cultures. Setting up a multicultural/anti-racist classroom library is essential. Students should have access to quality literature on a daily basis.

Involve the students in the daily routines of taking care of the classroom. Gradually introduce the various "jobs" that they can take. What does it mean to be a "leader"? How can they help to take attendance and get the lunch count in? Empower them to call others to line up, or to "control traffic" as children wait their turns. Table captains can oversee distribution and collection of materials. Add other tasks like holding doors, dispensing soap, watering plants, etc., and soon there will be enough work for everyone to have a specific job each day.

The trick is to "share" the power with your students in ways that benefit everyone. Don't be afraid to involve the kids in discussions about what might make your classroom better.

— Rita Tenorio

Do I have to spend my own money on classroom supplies?

Before I ran out to the nearest Office Depot, I always checked with colleagues to see if anything my students needed was already in the building. That helped keep me from spending my own money. In the "supply closet" I sometimes found pencils, rulers, scissors, and standard issue writing paper (a must for the early childhood teacher).

If you go to the teacher supply cupboard and discover it is bare (which has also been my experience at times), don't give up. One year my co-teacher and I drafted a letter introducing ourselves to the parents of our early-elementary students. It included a supply checklist for the school year: a 10-pack of #2 pencils, a 24-count box of crayons, half a dozen two-pocket folders, glue sticks, two boxes of tissues, a book bag, etc. We also specified what we didn't want: three-ring binders and the jumbo box of crayons were too bulky; markers were too messy!

We expected our students to all arrive with supplies, but we didn't assume they all would, so I created an emergency stash. First I went through all of the school supplies I'd collected from my own years in school, pulling out my old folders and pencils. Then I asked my sister for crayons and pencils that children weren't using any more. Thus I had a small cache of supplies for those children who came to school with nothing.

But that number was extremely low! Even my children whose families really struggled economically arrived that first week with something. Whatever the reason, none of my kids were ashamed, embarrassed, or doing without, and I was not charging boxes of Crayolas on my Visa card.

I also collected everything that we didn't need right away and put it in our community closet. That way it didn't clutter up desks or get used up needlessly or ruined. When a student needed a new homework folder, I knew where to find one.

— Stephanie Walters

ment straight. Various forms of record and grade books exist, but what I have found helpful is a clipboard with a sheet of mailing labels. This allows me to take notes on what children are doing and later peel off the label and put it into a three-ring binder of class observations and grades, which has a separate page for each student. Notes range from things such as "counting with fingers to solve problem" to "didn't seem to comprehend passage in independent book." These labels accumulate over time. Assuming I write neatly and in enough detail the first time, they're very helpful when it comes time to write report comments or during parent-teacher conferences. I also use this binder to note any parent contact or student conferences I have.

When more than one teacher is working directly with students, I have found that keeping a "running record" as a word processing file on a shared computer, or a shared file on a file server, is an excellent way to maintain joint records of student progress and contact.

Learning from Doing

Just as we expect our students to learn from their experiences, so should we. Thus spending a little time at the end of the day or week, or even at the end of the school year, to reflect on how to better organize and manage your classroom is worthwhile. Take some notes, keep a file on your computer titled "better ideas for next year" and write down ideas that might improve your teaching next year. ■

How I Survived
My First Year

It was a Friday afternoon and the end of my sixth-period freshman social studies class. As two of my students walked out the door, I overheard one say to the other: "Do you know what this class reminds me of? A local TV commercial."

It was a crushing comment. I knew exactly what she meant. It was my first year as a teacher. And as hard as I was working, the class still felt ragged, amateurish — well-intended, but sloppy. Her metaphor, invoking the image of a salesman trying too hard, was perfect.

As the last student filed out, the best I could do was remember the words of Lee Hays of the Weavers: "Like kidney stones and the Nixon presidency, this too will pass."

Twenty-five years later, there are still days when my class feels a bit like a local TV ad. But I continue to experiment, continue to study my own classroom practice. And looking back, I think I learned some things that first year that might be useful to pass on.

The first couple of years in the classroom establish what could be called a teacher's "professional trajectory." Most of us come out of college full of theory and hope. But then our lofty aims often bump up against the conservative cultures of our new schools, and students who often have been hardened by life and public schooling.

BY
BILL
BIGELOW

How we respond to this clash of idealism versus cynicism begins to create patterns that help define the teachers we'll become.

Which is not to say that the mistakes we make early on are repeated over and over throughout our careers. I probably did more things wrong than right my first year, and I'd like to think that I've grown since then.

Perhaps the best we can do is to ensure that early in our teaching lives we create mechanisms of self-reflection that allow us to grow, and allow us to continually rethink our curricula and classroom approaches. Nurturing these critical mechanisms may be vital if we're to maintain our hope in increasingly trying times.

My First Job

Year number one was not easy, as can be gathered from the incident described above. Typical of the cir-

VOICES FROM THE CLASSROOM

"I THINK NEW TEACHERS need a combination of the practical and the visionary. For survival purposes it's important to find people to share your experiences and struggles as you go through them. It's also important to find someone who can orient you to your school's strengths, weaknesses, and possibilities."

— Stan Karp

cumstances of most first-year teachers, principals did not line up to compete for my services. I began on the substitute list, and was lucky to land that spot. I know there are people who enjoy subbing: no papers to correct, no lesson plans to fret over, frequent changes of scenery, and so forth. But I hated it. I didn't know the kids' names; they often began in let's-terrorize-the-sub mode; teachers invariably left awful lesson plans ("Review chapter 20 and have them study for the test") but resented it if I didn't follow them to the letter; and I rarely had an opportunity to practice my craft: teaching.

Finally, in late October I did get a job — at Grant High School in Portland, Oregon, where I had completed my student teaching. It was a school with a diverse student body, about 30% African-American, with its European-American students drawn from both working class and "up on the ridge" neighborhoods. I had two preps: U.S. history and something called "freshman social studies" (and baseball coaching in the spring).

As I was to learn, I'd been hired to teach "overflow" classes, classes that had been formed because Grant's enrollment was much higher than expected. Teachers chose the "surplus" students they would donate to these new classes. Then the administration hired a sub to baby-sit while they sought permission from higher-ups to offer a contract to a regular teacher. In the meantime, the kids had driven two subs to quit. I was hired during the tenure of sub number three. My position was officially designated "temporary." In other words, I would automatically lose my job at the end of the year — unless another teacher fell ill, retired, died, quit, or had a baby.

My first meeting with the administrative team of principal, vice-principal, and curriculum specialist was perfunctory. I was told that "freshman social studies" meant one semester of career education, one semester of world geography, and no, they weren't sure which

SHOW THEM YOUR HUMANITY

The most useful piece of advice in the infancy of my career came from Tom McKenna, my cooperating teacher during my student teaching at Grant High School. It wasn't spoken advice, but he demonstrated it countless times in his classroom demeanor: Show the students that you love and respect them; play with them; joke with them; let them see your humanity. Good lesson plans are essential, yes, but ultimately students respond to the teacher as a human being.

Easier said than done, to be sure. Some days I would start out full of love and humor, but the students' surliness would defeat me by period's end. However, on better days, days when I had designed lessons that channeled rather than suppressed their fitful energy, or when I found some way to coax them to share their real stories — and thus I could share mine — I glimpsed the classroom life that was meant to be. We stopped being boss and workers, guard and inmates. The pictures of Molly, Tony, Tara, Tonya, Scott, Ken, Dee, et al. that I carry in my head are from those days.

— Bill Bigelow

came first. Nor did they know which, or even if, textbooks were used. But I could pick up my two-ream allotment of ditto paper from the department chair.

They gave me a key to Room 10 and sent me to review my "work station," as the principal, an ex-Navy man, called it. Room 10 was a runt: a tiny basement classroom crammed with 1950s-style student desks and a loud, hulking heating unit in the rear. But it was mine. It turned out students had been issued textbooks — for U.S. history, something like *God Bless America: We're Number One,* and for world geography, the cleverly titled *World Geography.*

Don't Be the Lone Ranger

Before the students, came the questions: Should I use these text-books? How do I grade? What kind of "discipline" policy should I have? How should I arrange the classroom? What do I teach on the first day?

My answers to these and other typical new-teacher questions are less important than the process of answering them. And this is perhaps the most valuable lesson I drew from that first year: Don't be the Lone Ranger. In September I had organized a study/support group with several teachers, some brand new, others with a few years of experience. We were united by a broad vision of creating lively and thoughtful classrooms where we provoked students to question the roots of social problems and encouraged them to believe that they could make a difference in the world. This group became my haven, offering comfort in times of stress — which was most of the time — and concrete advice to vexing questions.

(I don't mean to suggest that these support groups are only for the inexperienced. I've been in a study/action group, Portland Area Rethinking Schools, for many years, and this group and a sub-group aimed at sharing curriculum on global justice issues continue to offer essential support. They remind me that I'm not alone and they offer practical advice.)

We met weekly and usually divided our time between discussion of issues in education — tracking, discipline, teacher union politics, school funding, etc. — and specific classroom problems we encountered. Sometimes we brainstormed ideas for particular units people were developing: for example, Native-American history or the U.S. Constitution. It was also to this group that I brought complaints of rowdy classes and recalcitrant students, practical concerns about leading discussions or structuring a major project, and questions of how curricularly adventurous I could be without incurring the wrath of an administrator.

I'm a bit embarrassed to admit it, but I was glad that the group was composed mostly of teachers from other schools. Because of the huge gulf between my classroom ideals and my day-to-day practice, I felt somewhat ashamed and was reluctant to share my stumbles and doubts with more experienced colleagues in the building.

There were only eight of us in the group but we taught in four different districts; two were Title I teachers and three worked in alternative programs. The diversity of work situations yanked me out of the isolation of my classroom cubicle and forced me to see a bigger educational picture. Sheryl Hirshon's frequent despair with her Title I classes in a rural Oregon community may have been of a different sort than my frequent despair at urban Grant High School. But each of us could learn from how the other analyzed and confronted our difficult situations. (Sheryl ended up leaving teaching, moved to Nicaragua, taught for years in literacy programs there, and wrote the wonderful book about the 1979 literacy crusade, *And Also Teach Them to Read* [Lawrence Hill & Co., 1984].)

Occasionally our meetings turned into aimless whining sessions. But other times, a simple comment could remind us of our ideals and keep us on the path. I remember in a weak moment confessing that I was going to start relying on the textbook: I was just too tired, scrambling to create my own curriculum from scratch, re-typing excerpts from assorted books in the days before we teachers were allowed access to a copy machine, and when personal computers were still a thing of the future.

My friend Peter Thacker, sympathetic yet disapproving, simply asked: "Bill, do you really want to do that?"

OK, it bordered on a guilt trip. But that's all it took for me to remember that in fact I really didn't want to do that. The group was simultaneously collective conscience and inspiration.

Moving Beyond the Textbooks

Not all textbooks are so wretched, although as I recall mine were pretty awful. But as a beginning teacher I needed to see myself as a producer, not merely a consumer, of curriculum. It's hard work to translate the world into engaging lesson plans, but unless we're content to subordinate our classrooms to the priorities of the corporations that produce textbooks and other canned curricula, that's exactly what we have to do every day.

It's not that textbooks are a vast wasteland of corporate propaganda with no value whatsoever. I've borrowed lots of good ideas from textbook study guides. But they can easily narrow, distort, and misdirect our efforts.

To offer just one example: In *Lies My Teacher Told Me* (Touchstone, 1996), James Loewen's valuable critique of contemporary U.S. history textbooks, he demonstrates that all major texts downplay or totally ignore the history of the struggle against racism in the United States. Especially as a beginning teacher, if I had relied on textbooks to shape the outlines of my U.S. history curriculum, I would have neglected crucial areas of inquiry — and may never have realized it.

In addition to the support group, my planning book was another confidant of sorts. In it I would describe the activities I intended to do each week. Then I would record in some detail what actually happened. This was especially useful the following summer, when I could sit on the porch and leisurely flip through the book looking for patterns in students' responses to various lessons and teaching methods.

When I read back through that planning book today, I'm reminded of how helpless I often felt. From November 28, 1978, for example: "Things seem to be getting much rowdier in both my freshman classes. And I'm not sure exactly what to do." I wrote frequently about their

VOICES FROM THE CLASSROOM

"A TEACHER I WORKED with told me, 'One night at about 7 o'clock I was still working on a curriculum unit for *Sarah, Plain and Tall,* and I realized that all over the city other teachers were probably also developing lessons for the same book. It just didn't make sense.' And it doesn't. Establish a community of people who develop curriculum together. The work not only goes faster, but it's usually better because you have someone to talk through your ideas with."

— Linda Christensen

"groans." But having the journal to look back on after that first year also allowed me to search out the causes of the rowdiness and groans. I saw that my failure to engage them was more pronounced when I tried to pound them with information. My observations after a lecture on the roots of the Civil War were blunt, and a trifle pathetic: "People were very bored. I guess I should find another way to present it — even though it's interesting to me."

What's obvious to me now was not so obvious at the time: When students experience social dynamics from the inside — with role plays, stories, improvisations — they aren't so rowdy and they aren't so bored. There's a direct relationship between curriculum and "classroom management" that isn't always explicitly acknowledged in teaching-methods courses prospective teachers take.

The following year, I designed a simulation to get at the pre–Civil War sectional conflicts, and wrote a role play that showed students firsthand why Lincoln's election led to Southern secession. The role play also prompted students to think critically about the "Lincoln freed the slaves" myth. The point is simply that it was vital that I had some mechanisms to be self-reflective that first year.

(A wonderful book that helped me develop a more student-friendly, hands-on curriculum was *Changing Learning, Changing Lives,* by Barbara Gates, Susan Klaw, and Adria Steinberg [The Feminist Press, 1979]. Sadly, the book is long out of print, but you can often find a used copy through bookstores or Internet-based book finding services.)

Feeling Like a Jilted Lover

The principal made his one and only appearance in my classroom on March 15. Actually, he didn't come in, but knocked on the door and waited in the hallway. When I answered he handed me my official termination notice.

It was expected. I'd known I wouldn't be back because I was a temporary. But still there had been that slight hope. I guess by contract or law March 15 was the final date to notify teachers if they wouldn't be returning. I had about three months to let my unemployment sink in.

When that June date finally came, I packed my little white Toyota with the files, books, posters, and other knickknacks I'd accumulated throughout the year. I stood looking at the bare walls, my tiny oak desk, and Hulk the heater. And I left.

My tears didn't start until I was in the safety of my living room.

Tom McKenna, my cooperating teacher when I was a student teacher, had said that at the end of the year he always felt like a jilted lover. "Wait, there was more I wanted to say to you," he would think as the students filed out for the last time. And: "I always cared more about this than you did."

Sitting there on my couch, I now knew exactly what he meant. When it's over, you're left with the should-have-dones, the sense of missed opportunities, and the finality of it all. The end-of-the-year cry has become one of my worklife rituals: "There was more we had to say to each other."

The school district had made it clear that I was not guaranteed a job the following September. Thanks to this official non-guarantee I was able to collect unemployment that summer — in spite of the state functionary who told me with a sneer: "Unemployment benefits are not vacation pay for teachers, ya know."

But job or no job, benefits or no benefits, I'd made it. I'd finished my hardest year.

I would like to be able to say that the kids pulled me through. I always found that image of "young, idealistic superteacher and students versus hostile world" very appealing. And some years the kids did pull me through. But that first year, the more significant survival strategy was my reliance on a network of colleagues who shared a vision of the kind of classroom life, and the kind of world, we wanted to build.

That first year, we pulled each other through. ∎

Teaching for Social Justice

I t is a sad statement on the moral sensibility of our schools and society that one has to advocate for teaching for social justice. As one of my elementary school students once told me, "You know, Mr. Kohl, you can get arrested for stirring up justice."

One problem is that many people — children as well as adults — do not believe that justice is worth fighting for. One cannot assume an idea or cause will be embraced merely because it is just, fair, or compassionate. Contemporary society values self-interest and personal gain over compassion and the communal good.

So what are social justice teachers — those who care about nurturing all children and who are enraged at the prospect of students dying young, going hungry, or living meaningless and despairing lives — to do? How can they go against the grain and use their classrooms to work in the service of their students?

My suggestions are both pedagogical and personal.

First, don't teach against your conscience. Don't align yourself with texts, people, or rules that hurt children. Resist them as creatively and effectively as you can, whether through humor or by developing alternative curricula. Try to survive, but don't make your survival in a particular job the overriding determinant of

BY HERBERT KOHL

what you will or won't do. Don't become isolated or alone in your efforts; reach out to other teachers, community leaders, church people, and parents who feel as you do. Find a school where you can do your work and then stand up for the quality of your work. Don't quit in the face of opposition; make people work hard if they intend to fire or reprimand you for teaching equity and justice.

Second, hone your craft as a teacher. When I first began teaching, I jumped into struggles for social justice. During one of my efforts a community person asked: "So, what's going on in your classroom that's different than what you're fighting against? Can your students read and do math?" I had to examine my work, which was full of passion and effort but deficient in craft. I realized that I needed to take the time to learn how to teach well, or I couldn't extend myself with authority and confidence in organizing efforts. This is essential for caring teachers. We have to get it right for our own students or we can't presume to take on larger systems, no matter how terrible those larger systems are. As educators, we need to root our struggles for social justice in the work we do every day, in a particular community, with a particular group of students.

> **VOICES FROM THE CLASSROOM**
>
> "NEVER FORGET THAT YOUR passion for your students and your passion for justice are both worthy endeavors. Do not believe you need to forsake one for other. Stay true to your authentic self."
>
> — Dale Weiss

Third, look around at the many effective ways of teaching children. I don't believe there is a single technique or curriculum that leads to success. Consequently, pick and choose, retool and restructure the best of what you find and make it your own. Most of all, watch your students and see what works. Listen to them, observe how they learn, and then, based on your experience and their responses, figure out how to practice social justice in your classroom.

Fourth, it is not enough to teach well and create a social justice classroom separate from the larger community. You have to be a community activist, a good parent, a decent person, and an active community member as well.

Is all of this possible? Probably not. Certainly it isn't easy and often demands sacrifices. And at the end of the day it might also make you sad, because there is so much more that needs to be done, so many students who don't even have the advantage of a decent classroom and a caring teacher.

This leads to my final suggestion.

Protect and nurture yourself. Have some fun in your life; learn new things that only obliquely relate to issues of social justice. Teachers do a lot of work outside of school hours, yes, and you need to expect that. But daunting though it sounds, you also need to make time for yourself. Walk, play ball or chess, swim, fall in love. Don't forget how to laugh or feel good about the world. Have fun so that you can work hard; and work hard so that you and your students and their parents can have fun without looking over their shoulders.

This is not a question of selfishness but one of survival. Don't turn teaching for social justice into a grim responsibility, but take it for the moral and social necessity that it is. ■

The above is adapted from the afterward to *Teaching for Social Justice*, edited by William Ayers, Jean Ann Hunt, and Therese Quinn (New York: Teachers College Press, 1998). Reprinted with permission.

How Jury Duty
Saved My Career

I was so happy with my room. It looked great, if I did say so myself. The word wall was up, the second graders' nametags were all taped down, the first-day activities were all set out.

My teaching partner and I had met several times over the summer to create our plan for the new school year. We were both first-year teachers but we had become really good friends during the time we'd spent together planning our curriculum, and we were really looking forward to meeting and greeting our group of 30 kids.

We were in our room the day before our students were to arrive, rehearsing, when all my plans went straight out the window.

"Ms. Walters, I need to see you," the voice of our principal said over the PA system. Even as a teacher, being summoned to the principal's office made my heart sink a little.

It sank even more at her office. She told me that due to funding problems, our school couldn't afford to put two teachers in the second-grade classroom. And we hadn't been able to fill our opening in fifth grade. I was now assigned to teach fifth grade.

BY
STEPHANIE
WALTERS I was completely dumbfounded. In an instant I saw my diligent work for an entire summer erased. I had invested so many hours in creating a warm, nurturing environment conducive to learn-

ing and a well-rounded, appropriate curriculum — for second graders! I had nothing prepared for fifth graders. And they would be arriving tomorrow!

"So what now?" I asked my principal.

"I think you should go up to your new room and get ready for the students," she said, handing me a class list. She told me to work as a team with the other fifth-grade teacher. As I left she added: "Ms. Walters, this will be good for you. It's good to learn flexibility early in your career."

Before that meeting I had been an energetic and eager new teacher, facing a tremendous new challenge, yes, but with a plan in my head and a friend and colleague by my side in the classroom.

Now I was alone, and utterly unprepared. I suddenly felt tired, and scared.

An Audience with "The Queen"

I made my way to "my" room, opened the door and was totally depressed by what I saw. It was naked: nothing on the walls, not a pencil or a single sheet of paper in sight. The maintenance crew had stacked up the desks in one corner when they cleaned the carpets and they were still there in a big, looming pile.

I walked into the room in a fog. I couldn't help thinking about the second-grade classroom I had just left, and all the time and effort I had spent setting it up. I was supposed to start all over. And the kids were coming tomorrow.

I thought I'd start by arranging the room and making nametags. I looked at the class list. Only a handful of the 25 students were reading at or above grade level. Eight of them were students with special needs. I looked at the birth dates: Three had been retained. I really do have my work cut out for me, I thought. Can I do this?

I decided the nametags could wait. First I would introduce myself to my new teaching teammate, the other fifth-grade teacher. Maybe she could help me get started. She was known around our school as "The Queen." She was a good teacher and the principal often raved about her creative ideas in the classroom. But I had learned quickly that The Queen was regarded with great suspicion and cynicism by more than a few teachers in the building. They thought she was arrogant and treated people, students and teachers alike, with disdain. "Steer clear of The Queen," one colleague had warned me. "She's poison."

Unfortunately, this was not an option now. She was officially my partner.

I crossed the hall, knocked on her door and opened it. Her room was like day to my new room's night. Every wall was covered with brightly colored posters and charts. Her desks were neatly arranged and she had first-day activities ready and waiting for her students. She was leaning against her desk and smiled pleasantly as I walked in.

"Hi, Sandy," I said. "I just wanted to let you know I'm going to be the new teacher in the other fifth-grade room. And I thought you might have some tips for me."

"Oh, yeah, sure," she said, beckoning me in. She seemed nice enough. She told me about how she was setting up her room, what her standards were for her class, and what she would be doing with her students during the first few days. Then she gave me some puzzle sheets that my kids could do. "In down time," she suggested. I was starting to think I had this woman all wrong.

We had been talking for a while when she looked at her watch. "Oh, it's getting late and I have to pick my son up from my mom's," she said as she picked up the phone. "Let me just see if I can stay longer…. Hi, Mom, can I come and get Jake a little later? I have to stay late helping the new person in the other fifth-grade room. Yeah, she isn't really a teacher yet…."

She continued talking to her mom but I have no idea what she said. All I could hear was the blood pumping in my ears. I wasn't really a teacher? What kind of crack was that? I wanted to pull the phone out of her hand, take her by the wrist and march her down to see my beautiful second-grade classroom — the room that used to be mine,

VOICES FROM THE CLASSROOM

"TEACHING IS FULL OF successes and failures. Ultimately, although I spent sleepless nights worrying about my mistakes, I learned far more from my failures. You are going to fail throughout your teaching career. If you're not making mistakes, it means that you're not taking risks — you're not attempting new curriculum, new strategies. When you fail you have to reflect on what happened and learn from it."

— Linda Christensen

anyway. OK, I wanted to tell her, I'm not ready to teach fifth grade, but that's because I was transferred to the classroom across the hall from yours 20 minutes ago. It's not my fault.

But I didn't make a scene. Instead I sat there for a while longer, waiting for my next chance to escape without being too rude. Finally I headed back to my room, clutching my puzzle sheets, to start unstacking desks and to figure out what to do next.

"This Is Stupid!"

"Michael, Darrin, stop it right now!" I yelled.

It was two months later. The class was supposed to be working on an art project for open house. Soon two of my more active boys had begun to fling paint at each other. Sadly, this was nothing new. Michael and Darrin were constantly pestering other students and each other.

Any group project spelled danger. I had tried a number of times to put my students into cooperative groups, but they always degenerated into little nests of squabbling kids that didn't get much work done. Instead I'd taken to having the kids do individual exercises, which meant stacks and stacks of papers to correct at the end of every day.

In an effort to restore order I told the kids we were done with the art project and tried to get them working on response logs for a book we were reading. Anthony sat at his desk and refused to do any work. Mark also refused, and was very vocal about it. "This is stupid!" he said.

"Is there something else you want to do?" I asked him. I thought maybe I could engage Mark by tapping into something he would enjoy. But he was having none of it. "Nothing you could do," he snapped. "I hate this school and I hate this class. I want Miss Sheffer back!"

I'd heard that refrain before. Many of my students had been in Miss Sheffer's class in fourth grade, after they'd spent third grade with a teacher who called them names and insulted them. Miss Sheffer had been much nicer to them. But she had left before the school year ended, only to be replaced by sub after sub. Pretty soon it became a game for kids: How quickly could they run the new teacher out of the room?

I was determined not to let them do the same to me. But I was having problems. Why weren't my small-group activities working? Was I doing something wrong? I refused to give in to the cynical notion that the kids in my room were too wild to teach. But what could I do?

Now Mark was up and fighting again. I had to call the office and have him removed. During the commotion The Queen suddenly appeared in my doorway.

"Room 20, you have disturbed my class's silent reading," she said sharply. "What are you doing in here?" She surveyed the room, finally fixing her stare on me. "We'd appreciate your help so that we can read our books," she said. I wanted to melt into the floor.

Many times during the past two months I'd found myself running a race at the end of the school day, to get my kids on the bus and beat a retreat to the ladies' room before letting go of the tears that had been building all day. As The Queen turned on her heel and marched back to her own classroom, I knew today would be no different.

This was not the kind of input from colleagues I had been hoping for. Despite the principal's decree that The Queen and I form a team, I'd gotten very little support from her. There had been a few more stacks of puzzle sheets, but that was about it.

The school district had assigned me a mentor as well, an experienced teacher designated to provide support. I was one of perhaps 20 teachers she was driving from school to school to see. And while she'd been sympathetic, she hadn't been much help with my classroom practice either. It was November, and so she was bringing me handouts about the first Thanksgiving to pass around, with cute little cartoons of turkeys and Pilgrims. We hadn't had a single substantial discussion about teaching. I was still figuring this stuff out for myself.

I was not feeling well. I was tired all the time and I'd been sniffling for a couple of weeks, fighting a pitched battle with some kind of bug. I was always stuffed up and had a hard time hearing the kids. Plus, to make matters worse, now I was losing my voice. But I never dreamed of taking a sick day or making an doctor's appointment. I had not left my class with a substitute, ever. I was too afraid of what they would do.

I was arriving at school at 7 every morning, staying until 6, then going home to tackle an endless stack of individual worksheets. I never got them all done at school. Even when my kids were at art or gym the constant interruptions — from PA announcements to well-meaning colleagues who just wanted to drop by and chat — always kept me from making much headway.

I was always lugging stacks of papers home to correct on the kitchen table. For dinner I'd grab something out of the fridge or cook up a batch of popcorn and eat as I worked. At some point I'd push the papers aside and go to bed, inevitably feeling that I was still behind, and falling behind further still. And then the alarm would go off the next morning and I'd start all over again.

That night as I left school, I tried to take stock. Why was I such a bomb at this teaching thing? Why couldn't I get these kids to respond? And the big one: Why was I still hanging on?

As I drove home, I decided to quit. It's time to admit I'm in over my head, I thought. Give it up. Get a job as a political organizer, or maybe just go back to being a teacher's assistant. Let someone else take the lead in the classroom.

I got home, dumped the mail from my mailbox onto the kitchen table unread, and managed to get undressed before I dropped into bed. My mind was made up. I'd resign tomorrow.

The Letter

I woke up feeling not at all refreshed and began the familiar routine: shower, coffee, worry. Already my mind was racing: Who would get into a fight on the bus and show up in a bad mood? Who would mouth off to me, and how should I respond? My stomach swiftly twisted into all its familiar knots. Even knowing I was going to quit didn't temper my morning dread.

I slumped into a kitchen chair with my coffee cup and glanced down at the pile of mail I had tossed on the table the night before. There was a very official-looking envelope peeking out from under the credit card offers. "Official Jury Summons" was printed on the front.

Jury duty. I was being called for jury duty. A two day commitment. Two days away from my classroom.

As I examined the summons I thought things over. I knew I could probably get out of serving, but I decided not to try. Somehow leaving the school for a few days to do my civic duty was easier to justify than, say, leaving to go see a doctor about my stuffed-up head. It seemed less selfish, I guess. Besides, I told myself, I'm ready to quit. Maybe jury duty will buy me some time away from the job to rethink my options.

It was a week before my time to serve came up, a week during which all the same terrible things happened to me at school: kids fighting, papers piling up, that sting of failure dogging my steps, the tears welling up inside me as I made my way through the day. I didn't really think two days away from school would change my mind about quitting. But I resolved to hang in there and see what jury duty would bring. Just be patient, I told myself, and get this week over with.

An Amazing Day

The day finally came. I parked in the special free garage for jurors, walked into the courthouse and headed through the doors marked "Jurors Only." It was the first time in months I'd felt like I was being treated special.

I gave my summons to the attendant and she told me to have a seat, they would be calling me shortly. I found a chair and dropped my bulging briefcase next to it with a thud. It was crammed with uncorrected tests and answer sheets I was determined to finish during the next two days.

I settled into my chair and looked around at my fellow jurors-to-be. Some were reading novels, a couple were knitting. One man was doing a crossword. I felt a surge of jealousy. I've always loved crosswords, but I couldn't remember the last time I'd done one. I should be doing a crossword puzzle right now instead of correcting these papers, I thought.

I opened my briefcase and got started. And then, an amazing thing happened. As the wheels of justice turned slowly around me, leaving me completely alone, I corrected every single paper in my case. It took a couple of hours but I never felt overwhelmed. I just did it. When I was done I sat there, trying to figure out why my work hadn't once come this easily since the school year began.

I realized this was the first time I had been able to spend a significant chunk of time grading papers early in the day, instead of trying to tack the chore on to the end of 11 grinding hours at school. And there had been no distractions, no PA system going off every few minutes, no friendly visitors looking to chew the fat.

I was done with my schoolwork! I felt positively giddy as I got up from my chair to get a newspaper. A newspaper! My chance to do a crossword had come a lot sooner than I'd thought.

The paper kept me occupied until lunch. And then an even more amazing thing happened. When I came back to the waiting room I was told my services would no longer be required. My obligation had been met. I was free to go. I had a day and a half to myself.

Walking back to my car, I literally did not know what to do. I briefly considered going back to school. Maybe I should check on my room, see how the substitute was doing. Or maybe I could sneak in, find some more student work to bring home and sneak out again.

But no, something was happening to me. As I hefted my briefcase full of graded work, I felt some of my old confidence coming back. For the first time in a while I had some spring in my step. I decided I needed some time to think about this, to figure out what had been missing in my life these past few months, and how to get it back.

So instead of going back to work I went home, changed my clothes and took a walk. It was only for an hour, but I savored every stride of it. I felt free. As the knots in my leg muscles beginning to unbunch, I realized just how tight my whole body had become, how little exercise I'd had. I hadn't been getting out like this. Lately all my running had been done on the treadmill my principal dropped me onto the day I was re-assigned. I had been pumping away as hard as I could, head down, all alone, afraid to slow down or look around, and never seeming to get anywhere. It had gotten so bad that I'd been ready to quit teaching altogether.

Now, feeling a little looser and a lot less anxious, I realized I could stick it out. I had gotten back in touch with some of my strength. I didn't have to leave teaching. Instead I needed to figure out what was wrong and work on that.

Looking back it seems crazy that jury duty made such a big difference in my life path. But that's how it happened. If I hadn't found that summons in my mail that morning, I would have walked straight into the principal's office and quit.

> ## VOICES
> ### FROM THE CLASSROOM
>
> I THOUGHT, 'HEY, IT'S NOT going to be that hard to get the kids to like me. It's all going to be cool.' But it turned out to be the farthest thing from what I could have expected. In fact, one day I got in my car and started crying. I was like, 'Boy, they hate me.' But what I learned was it's not about being liked. It's about being trusted. And because I move close to 700 kids through my room in a week, it takes time to get to know them on a personal level, to learn what's happening in their lives. And until I have that information, I will never fully have their trust."
>
> — Steve Vande Zande

A New Game Plan

Five years later I was still a teacher, still hanging in there, even feeling proud of myself most days for the job I was doing. I kept my promise to myself to get off that treadmill and stay off.

Here — with the benefit of 20-20 hindsight — are some things I found it helpful to think about, things that I believe can help you stay in teaching for the long haul:

Take care of yourself. Shortly after jury duty I finally took a day off and went to the doctor for my stuffed-up head, and learned I had a double ear infection. A few doses of antibiotics later, I was as good as new. I shudder when I think of how long I went without seeing a doctor, all those days I struggled to hear what my kids were saying, what might have happened if I'd never been treated. That episode taught me: Pay attention to your body. If you're sick, get the treatment you need. Rest when you're tired.

Eat right. Popcorn is not a well-balanced dinner. It doesn't give your body what it needs. Neither does a steady diet of fat-laden fast food. You don't need to indulge in a macrobiotic seven-course meal every day, but you do need to make sure you're eating properly, getting enough protein, and consuming enough fruits and veggies to supply your body with what it needs to keep running properly. A few small changes in how you deal with food can go a long way. I started making big pots of beans or soup on Sunday to take for lunch during the week. It's a habit I continue today.

Get some exercise. You don't have to run marathons, but putting your body to work on a regular basis will help you release the tension that builds up during the workday.

Pace yourself on the job. Teaching is hard work, and even when you feel you're on the right track the hours can be long, the tasks many. Unless you consciously maintain a reasonable pace for yourself, you won't last long. Don't spend forever at school. Set reasonable limits and when you reach them, stop. That way you'll be strong when it's time to come back.

Don't expect to be perfect. Teaching is not easy. You're going to make mistakes. The trick is to learn from them, and to be forgiving of yourself as you do. It's part of the job to examine your teaching practice, maybe even fret over it a little, in pursuit of doing it better tomorrow. I have friends who've been teaching for 20 years, and I see them struggling in ways I once thought only new teachers struggled:

there's one kid in their class they're not sure how to reach, they wonder if they're on target with the message they're trying to deliver, etc. That kind of reflection comes with the territory. Don't let it consume you, but don't fear it either.

Find people who can help you. I realize now that one of my biggest problems when I started teaching fifth grade was a lack of professional support. I got puzzle sheets from The Queen and cute cartoons from my district-assigned mentor, but no real insight into what I was doing in the classroom and what was going wrong.

Now I know there was a reason all my cooperative learning activities failed: No one had ever taught my students how to work cooperatively. And I wasn't teaching them how either, just assigning them work to do as a group and turning them loose. What I needed to do was back up and spend some time with the kids on the specifics of working in a group, and to let them practice the necessary skills. Then maybe my group art projects wouldn't have turned into paint fights quite so quickly. And I wouldn't have felt the need to hand out so many individual worksheets, which left me staggering under the load of all those papers to correct.

As a new teacher, I was not prepared to address practice-related questions like that. Simply put, I didn't know what I didn't know. And I wasn't getting any insight from the people assigned to help me. I found I couldn't rely on them. I needed to seek people out, pick their brains, see what they could teach me.

Start with the other teachers in your building. Contact your union to see what kinds of support or enrichment they might offer. And seek out kindred spirits and talented teachers elsewhere in your community. Are there groups doing political work, for example, that are likely to attract other teachers who might share your interests? Does your union offer professional development activities?

Keep your classroom work relevant to kids' lives. Students are a lot more likely to act up when they're bored. You can address this somewhat by paying attention to your teaching methods: For example, don't just stand by the board and lecture all day. But another critical question to ask yourself frequently is: Are my students learning things that are meaningful to them? Are they being asked to memorize dry facts they will never need again after this class? Or are they being given a chance to learn about things that matter, that have bearing on their lives? This is a very big topic, which is discussed in more depth elsewhere in this book (for example, see "The Best Discipline Is Good Curriculum," page 185, and "Curriculum Is Everything That Happens," page 79). Keep it in mind as you work on curriculum and how you deliver it.

Do what you can to improve new teacher training. Once you've found your feet, start working with your school or your union to ensure that other new teachers get meaningful training and support. While it's true my mentor wasn't much help, she could have been, if she'd been able and willing to engage me in a real discussion of my teaching practice. Find out who is offering enrichment programs for teachers in your district and let them know what you would find helpful, what kind of support would help you most in examining and improving your practice. ■

All students' names have been changed.

12 Tips for New Teachers

I was 38 when I started my teaching career, and I thought I knew everything I needed to know. I'd been a community and union activist for years and I'd been political all my life. I figured all I had to do was bring my experience and politics to the classroom and I'd be a great teacher.

Was I wrong. Now I've been teaching high school for more than 13 years and I continue to be humbled. When I work with new teachers, I give them the following suggestions:

1 **Keep calm in all situations.** Calmness allows you to make rational decisions. If a student is confrontational or out of control, it never ever works to react with anger. Getting into a tug-of-war over who has the last word exacerbates the situation. Let the situation cool down and then try to have a mature conversation with those involved.

2 **Make respect central to your classroom culture.** A common expression I hear from my students and parents is: "You have to give respect to get respect." They're right. The only way to hold students to high and rigorous expectations is to gain their respect and their acknowledgment that your class will lead to real learning that will benefit them.

BY
LARRY
MILLER

3 **Base your curriculum on social justice.** Frame it with a critical edge. I have four questions for assessing my curriculum:

- Does the curriculum deepen students' understanding of social justice?
- Is the curriculum rigorous?
- Are students learning the skills they need to be critical thinkers, advance their education, be prepared for employment, and become active citizens?
- I am also now forced to ask the question: Does the curriculum increase students' ability to do well on state-mandated standardized tests?

4 **Keep rules to a minimum but enforce them.** Always have clear consequences and never threaten to take a particular action if you are not willing to carry it out. Talk to students as mature young adults.

5 **Whenever possible, connect your classroom discussions and curriculum to students' lives, community, and culture.** Learn as much as you can about your students. For example, I use hip-hop lyrics as a means to discuss current trends of thought and world views in my Citizenship class. Rappers offer plenty to discuss, both positive and negative. I get lyrics from the Internet, I borrow CDs from students, and I search for positive rap on TV and the radio.

6 **Learn from other teachers and staff.** Pay special attention to teachers and staff whose cultures and backgrounds are different from yours. I've always made a point of consulting every day with my colleagues. Their insight can be invaluable.

7 **Build students' confidence in their intelligence and creativity.** I've often heard my students call kids from the suburbs or those in AP classes "the smart kids." Don't let that go unchallenged. I start the year talking about "multiple intelligences" and how "being smart" can take many forms. I find daily examples of students' work and views to talk about as smart and intelligent.

8 **Distinguish between students' home language and their need to know "standard" English.** Work with both. This is a huge topic, one you will be dealing with throughout your career.

(For a more thorough discussion of home language see Linda Christensen's book *Reading, Writing, and Rising Up: Teaching About Social Justice and the Power of the Written Word,*which is described on page 68.)

9 Keep lecturing short. Have students regularly doing projects, reading, giving presentations, engaging in discussions, debating, doing role plays, and taking part in simulations.

10 Have engaging activities prepared for students when they walk into the classroom. I might play a piece of music, put an African expression on the board to interpret, or put students in "critical thinking groups" to solve a puzzle.

11 Call students' homes regularly both for positive and negative reports. Visit their homes. Students often belong to non-school organizations. For example, during Black History Month many churches in the black community have special programs that students perform in. Attend, and go to other presentations given by groups they belong to.

12 Mobilize students to join in new experiences. For example, I sponsor a "polar bear club": We jump into Lake Michigan to celebrate New Year's Day, then we all eat breakfast together. ■

Confronting
White Privilege

As an educator of European descent, it has always been important to me to understand the impact that being white has on
the way I view the world, the lens through which I create and
implement my lesson plans, and the ways in which I react towards my
students and the world views they bring to school with them.

Before entering the teaching profession, I worked in a variety of
ways on issues of social justice. Through this work I realized that
questioning what it means to be white in U.S. society and examining
the privileges afforded to me because of my skin color are part of a lifelong journey. Three particular incidents stand out as turning points.

A Lesson from the Women's Movement

The first was almost 25 years ago. I was a relatively new political activist,
living in the Pacific Northwest, who had become involved through the
women's movement. I was young, idealistic, and enthusiastic.

During this period I was involved with a variety of women's concerns, including affirmative action, pro-choice activism, and employment issues. While attending a conference on
women's prison reform, I participated in a session
called "Who's Running the Women's Movement?" I
assumed, naïvely, that the only logical answer was

BY
DALE
WEISS

women. But several women of color at the session said they felt the women's movement was not inclusive to women of color. They said that all women in positions of leadership within the movement were white and that both the leadership and broader membership were unwilling to address issues of racism head on.

I didn't understand what they were getting at. I was defensive and confused. From my perspective, the women's movement clearly addressed issues of concern to women of color. After all, didn't issues of affirmative action, reproductive rights, and employment concern and affect women of color as well? It was true, I thought, that the women I worked with were all white, but we were honest individuals who sincerely cared about ending racism. It puzzled me that our intentions could be questioned. It seemed to me that if women of color didn't feel included in the women's movement, that was their problem.

Yet, I was haunted by their accusations. I couldn't forget them.

Wanting to make sense of the comments by the women of color, I became involved with the National Anti-Racist Organizing Committee, a national multi-ethnic organization committed to addressing racism through education and community action. I slowly learned to examine racism not solely as the result of individual actions or intentions, but rather as a systemic institutional problem involving issues of power. It suddenly became clearer that, for the most part, white people were in positions of power, which often included making decisions on behalf of — but not with or under the leadership of — people of color.

I regretted my arrogance toward the women of color at the prison conference. I began asking myself questions: Did I understand the plight of the imprisoned women of color on whose behalf I was working? What did it mean to be part of a women's movement when the women in leadership were all middle-class whites? Can white people really know what is best for people of color?

I wanted to believe that all my work on issues of social justice somehow had elevated me above acting in ways that were blind to the experiences and perspectives of people of color. I wanted to believe that I — as someone committed to the women's movement — understood the reality of people of color as well as I understood the reality of people of European descent. I wanted to believe that the women of color at the prison conference were wrong. But no matter how hard I tried to believe these things, I knew my attempts served only to stall the internal work I needed to do. My journey of looking my own white privilege squarely in the face had clearly begun.

My attempts at answering my many questions became an internal battle that made me increasingly aware of white privilege. The more I learned, the more I became overwhelmed with guilt at being white. What had always seemed so "normal" was now something I wanted to reject. For the next several years I worked on justice issues confronting African Americans, Native Americans, Nicaraguans, and Salvadorans. Feeling so much guilt about being white, more than anything I wished I could "be" a person of color. Though I knew this was ultimately impossible, I mistakenly thought this would protect me from taking advantage of what it means to be white. I had no idea what it might mean to be both white and an anti-racist ally of people of color.

Looking Through the Lens of Race

Throughout the next several years, I continued to work with a variety of groups that addressed racism. My feelings of guilt for being white lessened and a deeper understanding of racism began to grow. Then in the mid-1980s my "newfound understanding" was again greatly challenged, providing my second major turning point.

I was working as a substitute teacher at a childcare center in Seattle that was created and run collectively by a racially diverse group of women and men. Pedagogically, the center fostered multicultural, anti-racist, non-sexist education. The children included African-American, Latino, white, and biracial children from a variety of family structures. The center's employment bylaws included a commitment that the staff mirror the diverse racial and gender makeup of the children. I found working there to be incredibly refreshing and inspirational.

I substituted daily at the center and both staff and parents appreciated my work. After several months, I applied for a staff opening, but in order to maintain racial balance among the staff, the center hired an African-American woman instead.

Intellectually, I understood the decision. But emotionally, this was something new for me. I had never before been denied employment because of my race. At times in the past it had been difficult for me to secure some jobs because I was a woman: For example, when I wanted to work as a laborer at the local bus company, I was hired only reluctantly, and thus became the first woman to ever do that job. But I had never faced a challenge securing employment because I was white. My experiences and observations had taught me that if white people — particularly men — set their sights on something, it could be theirs.

I was forced to look at life, and live it, through the lens of race. As I thought my situation through I realized I had not experienced some form of "reverse discrimination." Rather, the center was sticking to its principles by trying to keep staff diversity in synch with the diversity of students. This was neither preferential treatment to people of color nor discrimination against whites.

I also realized that I could not believe in these principles only when they did not directly affect me. I knew it was right that I had not been hired.

A few months later, a white woman on the center's staff resigned. A staff opening was posted for a white female. It was then that I was hired.

This was the first time I realized that "walking my talk" meant doing more than saying the correct words or taking a stand against racism only when it was convenient to do so. I began to realize that being an anti-racist activist meant connecting what I believed with how I acted, regardless of how that might personally affect me.

Through the center I began to understand how I, as a white woman, could work with other white people and people of color on the issue of racism. I came to realize there was nothing inherently wrong about being white. Rather, the issue was whether I chose to gain or accept advantage due to the color of my skin, or chose instead to work to eliminate racist practices that perpetuated the advantage. Working at the center helped me realize that fighting racism is not just a job for people of color acting on behalf of "their cause." It's also the responsibility of white people to speak out against racism and work toward its eradication.

Rejecting the Option to Retreat

My work with preschool-age children sparked my interest in getting a teaching license, which led to my third turning point.

My first teaching assignment was in a small town north of Seattle whose population was 98% white. My class consisted of 23 first graders, all white except for one African-American girl. I was committed to infusing my curriculum with a sense of justice and an anti-bias perspective. It was important to me to help my students gain an understanding of the many inequities that exist within our city, country, and world. Also, I wanted them to know there is always something that can be done — even by 6- and 7-year-olds — to make the world a more just place. Throughout the year I raised issues of race and ethnicity, gender, family diversity, class, and people with physical and/or mental challenges.

My students seemed to have an innate sense of fairness and were eager to address issues such as how to make the world a better place. But most other staff members did not share my commitment to anti-bias teaching, especially on matters of race.

At a staff meeting, I said I thought it was important that black history be celebrated throughout the school year, not just during Black History Month. A sixth-grade teacher responded by calling me a "nigger lover."

I was stunned. I asked him what he meant. "Exactly what I said," he replied.

Another teacher piped in: "I think what he's trying to say is that we don't have very many of those children at our school. So it's not really necessary to change things around to meet their needs. When I pull out my January/February box, there are pictures of Martin Luther King on my bulletin boards, along with pink cupids and red hearts. We don't need to put up pictures of Martin Luther King all year any more than we need to put up

---

VOICES FROM THE CLASSROOM

"IT'S HARD TO GET THE teachable moment. But when you get it, it's amazing. One time one of the kids looked at a piece of artwork and said, 'Oh, that's gay.' And another kid walked up to him and said, 'Well, that can't be gay because it's not alive.' That turned into a whole discussion about whether being gay is a choice. These things come up and they need to be discussed. And it's my role to make sure the kids know they are safe to express themselves. I realize it's very hard to drop things that have to get done if you have a deadline. But you have to — even if it means giving up class time or prep time to do it."

— Steve Vande Zande

pink cupids and red hearts all year."

I was no longer stunned. Now I was enraged. How could these teachers equate Valentine's Day with honoring black history? I also felt helpless. What could I do to counter such attitudes?

Part of me wanted to simply retreat, to drop the issue and thus "be safe." But another part of me was saying, "That's the point. You, as a white person, can retreat. People of color never can."

It was a moment of transformation for me. I realized I would always be perceived as a white person, and that people in the majority culture would always make assumptions about my beliefs based on my skin color. More than ever I realized that if I hid my beliefs about racism, I'd be exercising privilege as a white person. To be an antiracist, I had to be open about my beliefs.

Despite the lack of support from other staff, I continued with plans to introduce a study of black history to my students. It was difficult to find materials, so I decided to make a video on the topic with my students, entitled "Black History as Seen Through the Eyes of First Graders." The video was a compilation of original writings, artwork, and music, through which my students shared their thoughts and feelings as they began to understand racism through both historic and current events.

When the video was completed, we held a gala premiere for my students' parents, who were quite proud of their children's work. But the following day an anonymous note appeared in my school mailbox, apparently from a teacher. It read: "Do you also care about whether your students understand white history?" Once again I realized I had underestimated how threatening it can be to raise issues of race.

Though I had strong support from my kids' parents and the school's administration, my day-to-day conflicts with other staff members continued. In hindsight, I realize I should have paid more attention to building support among my colleagues. For example, I could have worked harder at collaborating with them in ways that were less threatening: I could have teamed up with another class to do the standard unit on dinosaurs, or tried creating a "buddy classroom" with one of the teachers at the intermediate level.

It was a painful, hard-learned lesson.

The Journey Continues

I left Seattle and went to work for the Milwaukee Public Schools. As I look back, and forward, I find that my journey to better understand racism and white privilege is far from over. Increasingly I find myself dealing with issues of race and racial privilege, not only as a white person but also as a Jew who experiences various forms of anti-Semitism. What does it mean to be a person who experiences both privilege and discrimination? It is a question I continue to try and answer.

And as an educator, I realize that my journey toward understanding racism will never be complete. For example, I want to move beyond multicultural education as it is commonly understood and take up not only diversity but racism, power, and privilege. Some days, this is easier than others.

I know that these issues will not be resolved in my lifetime. The real hope lies in grappling with such problems, and in creating future generations that do not feel threatened by issues of social justice but instead embrace the challenge of creating a better world. ∎

Other Resources From Rethinking Schools

Founded by classroom teachers and community activists in 1986, Rethinking Schools publishes and distributes a collection of books on important school issues, and a quarterly journal that remains the only publication of its kind edited by practicing classroom teachers.

For more information on these publications — including tables of contents, sample articles, and information about ordering online — visit our website at www.rethinkingschools.org. And while you're there, check out everything the website has to offer: articles from past issues of the journal, excerpts from our books, a searchable index, and special collections on important education topics such as school vouchers, sex education, and teaching about war.

Rethinking Schools — The Journal

This independent quarterly is written by teachers, parents, and education activists — people who understand the day-to-day realities of reforming our schools. Every issue is filled with innovative teaching ideas, analyses of important policy issues, and listings of valuable resources.

Rethinking Our Classrooms, Volume 1:
Teaching for Equity and Justice

Rethinking Our Classrooms begins where most school reforms never go: inside the classroom. This 208-page book includes creative teaching ideas, compelling narratives, and hands-on examples of how teachers can promote values of community, justice, and equality — and build academic skills. *Rethinking Our Classrooms* includes more than 75 articles, essays, poems, reproducible handouts, lesson plans, and resource lists. Nowhere is the connection between critical teaching and effective classroom practice made clearer or more accessible.

Rethinking Our Classrooms, Volume 2:
Teaching for Equity and Justice

This companion volume to *Rethinking Our Classrooms, Volume 1,* presents a rich new collection of from-the-classroom articles, curriculum ideas, lesson plans, poetry, and resources — all grounded in the realities of school life.

Rethinking School Reform: Views from the Classroom, edited by Linda Christensen and Stan Karp

Rethinking School Reform puts classrooms and teaching at the center of the debate over how to improve public schools. This collection of essays and articles offers a primer on a broad range of pressing issues, including school vouchers and funding, multiculturalism, standards and testing, teacher unions, bilingual education, and federal education policy.

Rethinking School Reform examines how various reform efforts promote — or prevent — the kind of teaching that can bring equity and excellence to all our children, and it provides compelling, practical descriptions of what such teaching looks like.

Rethinking Globalization: Teaching for Justice in an
Unjust World, edited by Bill Bigelow and Bob Peterson

This comprehensive 402-page book helps teachers raise critical issues with students in fourth through twelfth grades about the increasing globalization of the world's economies and infrastructures, and the many different impacts this trend has on our planet and those who live here. *Rethinking Globalization* offers an extensive collection of readings and source material on critical global issues, plus teaching ideas, lesson plans, and resources for classroom teachers.

Reading, Writing, and Rising Up: Teaching About Social Justice and the Power of the Written Word, by Linda Christensen

"My students walk out the school door into a social emergency," Linda Christensen writes. "I believe that writing is a basic skill that will help them both understand that emergency and work to change it." This practical, inspirational book offers essays, lesson plans, and a remarkable collection of student writing, all rooted in an unwavering focus on language arts teaching for justice.

Rethinking Columbus: The Next 500 Years, edited by Bill Bigelow and Bob Peterson

Why rethink Christopher Columbus? Because the Columbus myth is a foundation of children's beliefs about society. Columbus is often a child's first lesson about encounters between different cultures and races. The murky legend of a brave adventurer tells children whose version of history to accept, and whose to ignore. It says nothing about the brutality of the European invasion of North America. *Rethinking Columbus* offers more than 90 essays, poems, interviews, historical vignettes, and lesson plans packed with useful teaching ideas for kindergarten through college.

Transforming Teacher Unions: Fighting for Better Schools and Social Justice, edited by Bob Peterson and Michael Charney

This stimulating 144-page anthology looks at exemplary practices of teacher unions from the local to the national level. The 25 articles weave together issues of teacher unionism, classroom reform, working with local communities, and social justice. It challenges the reader, while presenting stirring new visions of teacher unions for the 21st century.

Failing Our Kids: Why the Testing Craze Won't Fix Our Schools, edited by Kathy Swope and Barbara Miner

The long arm of standardized testing is reaching into every nook and cranny of education. Yet relying on standardized tests distorts student learning, exacerbates inequities for low-income students and students of color, and undermines true accountability. *Failing Our Kids* includes more than 50 articles that provide a compelling critique of standardized tests and also outline alternative ways to assess how well our children are learning.

The Real Ebonics Debate: Power, Language, and the Education of African-American Children, edited by Theresa Perry and Lisa Delpit

The Oakland school board's now-infamous 1996 resolution recognizing Ebonics as a valid linguistic system generated a brief firestorm of hostile criticism and misinformation, then faded from public consciousness. But in U.S. classrooms the question of how to engage the distinctive language of many African-American children remains urgent. In *The Real Ebonics Debate,* some of our most important educators, linguists, and writers — as well as teachers and students reporting from the field — examine the lessons of the Ebonics controversy and unravel complexities of the issue that have never been widely acknowledged.

Rethinking Schools: An Agenda for Change, edited by David Levine, Robert Lowe, Bob Peterson, and Rita Tenorio

Published by The New Press, this is a collection of the most compelling, useful, and enduring work that has appeared in the journal *Rethinking Schools.*

Classroom Crusades: Responding to the Religious Right's Agenda for Public Schools

This collection of articles examines efforts by right-wing ideologues and activists to influence — and in some cases eliminate — our nation's public schools. Topics include sex education, creationism vs. evolution, school vouchers, and censorship.

Funding for Justice: Money, Equity, and the Future of Public Education, edited by Stan Karp, Robert Lowe, Barbara Miner, and Bob Peterson

A valuable, practical resource on an issue that touches every school and community. Going beneath the legal jargon and complex funding formulas, *Funding for Justice* presents complicated issues of school finance in a reader-friendly way for teachers and parents as well as policymakers and education advocates.

Selling Out Our Schools: Vouchers, Markets, and the Future of Public Education, edited by Robert Lowe and Barbara Miner

This book covers the major issues surrounding school vouchers and efforts to privatize our public schools and make them beholden to the marketplace. More than 35 articles by nationally respected educators and policymakers explain how vouchers and marketplace approaches to education threaten our basic concepts of equality and opportunity. ∎

Another 24 Terrific Books

ere are some additional works *not* published by Rethinking Schools. You don't have to run out and buy them all and read them in the next month, but when you get to them, you will find them invaluable.

Anti-Bias Curriculum: Tools for Empowering Young Children, by Louise Derman-Sparks and the A.B.C. Task Force (Washington, DC: National Association for the Education of Young Children, 1989).

Perhaps the best book for the early child/primary level on how to teach about all forms of bias and what to do about it.

Beyond Heroes and Holidays: A Practical Guide to K-12 Anti-Racist, Multicultural Education and Staff Development, edited by Enid Lee, Deborah Menkart, and Margo Okazawa-Rey (Washington, DC: Network of Educators on the Americas, 1998).

A 463-page treasury that includes lesson plans and staff development activities, as well as critical examinations of controversial school issues such as bilingual education and tracking. Contains an extensive guide to teaching and learning resources and many helpful Internet sites.

City Kids, City Teachers: Reports from the Front Row, edited by William Ayers and Patricia Ford (New York: New Press, 1996).

A provocative collection of 25 essays that explodes stereotypical myths about students in urban schools and provides many examples of big-city schools and teachers who are successful.

Creative Resources for the Anti-Bias Classroom, by Nadia Saderman Hall (Independence, KY: Delmar Thomson Learning, 1998).

This excellent book connects developmental skills for young children with the elements of an anti-bias curriculum. It's a resource that helps new teachers know where to begin infusing a more critical focus.

Crossing Over to Canaan: The Journey of New Teachers in Diverse Classrooms, by Gloria Ladson-Billings (San Francisco: Jossey-Bass, 2001).

Arguing that most teacher-education programs don't do enough to promote "culturally relevant pedagogy," Ladson-Billings recalls her own experiences as a new teacher and relates the trials and successes of participants in Teach for Diversity, an experimental graduate program at the University of Wisconsin–Madison which recruited teacher-trainees with a strong commitment to social justice and equality.

A Different Mirror: A History of Multicultural America, by Ronald Takaki (Boston: Little, Brown & Co., 1993).

Beginning with the colonization of the "New World" and ending with the Rodney King riots in Los Angeles in 1992, this book recounts U.S. history in the voices of Native Americans, African Americans, Jewish Americans, Irish Americans, Asian Americans, Latinos, and others. Takaki turns the Anglocentric historical viewpoint inside-out and examines the ultimate question of what it means to be an American.

De Colores Means All of Us: Latina Views for a Multi-Colored Century, by Elizabeth Martinez (Cambridge, MA: South End Press, 1998).

Martinez's 30-plus years of experience in the movements for civil rights, women's liberation, and Latina/Latino empowerment are reflected in these readable essays. She is particularly good on the struggles of Mexican Americans.

Flirting or Hurting? A Teacher's Guide on Sexual Harassment in Schools for 6th through 12th Grade Students, by Nan Stein and Lisa Sjostrom (Washington, DC: National Education Association, 1994).

This is a widely used, teacher-friendly curriculum with stories and role plays.

I Won't Learn from You: The Role of Assent in Learning,
by Herbert Kohl (Minneapolis: Milkweed, 1991).

Kohl argues that "refusal to learn," often viewed by teachers as failure, is actually a strategy of self-preservation against a school system that students perceive as racist, prejudiced, disrespectful or exclusionary. Teachers must begin, he says, by acknowledging these conditions as they work to win students' trust.

Lies My Teacher Told Me: Everything Your American History Textbook Got Wrong, by James W. Loewen (New York: Touchstone, 1996).

Loewen's book is an entertaining and eye-opening de-mything of key aspects of American history. It's both an effective critique of some of the most widely used history texts and an alternative history text in its own right.

The Light in Their Eyes: Creating Multicultural Learning Communities, by Sonia Nieto (New York: Teachers College Press, 1999).

Nieto takes us beyond individual learners to discuss the social context of learning, the history and manifestations of educational equity, the influence of culture on learning, and critical pedagogy. Centering on multicultural education as a transformative process, this book includes reflections of teachers who have undergone this process.

Open Veins of Latin America: Five Centuries of the Pillage of a Continent, 25th anniversary edition, by Eduardo Galeano (New York: Monthly Review Press, 1998).

This book vividly portrays the repeated invasion and subjugation of Latin America by political and monetary interests in Europe and the United States, as part of the crusade to build "the foundation stone upon which the giant industrial capital of modern times was built."

A Pedagogy for Liberation: Dialogues on Transforming Education, with Ira Shor and Paulo Freire (Westport, CT: Bergin and Garvey, 1986).

Two internationally acclaimed educators speak passionately about the role of education in various cultural and political arenas. They compare the problems facing education systems with those facing society as a whole, and argue for the transformation of classrooms so that students will think critically.

A People's History of the United States: 1492–Present, by Howard Zinn (New York: Perennial Classics, 2003).

The best single-volume history of the United States. No teacher should be without a copy. Some sections are readable by high school students.

The Power in Our Hands: A Curriculum on the History of Work and Workers in the United States, by Bill Bigelow and Norm Diamond (New York: Monthly Review Press, 1988). (Available from Rethinking Schools at www.rethinkingschools.org.)

A thoughtful collection of lessons and handouts extremely useful for engaging middle and high school students on labor history.

The Power of Their Ideas: Lessons for America from a Small School in Harlem, by Deborah Meier (Boston: Beacon Press, 2002).

A noted educator reflects on her successes and challenges working at Central Park East Secondary School, which earned a reputation for innovation and for encouraging high levels of student achievement. Meier's work emphasizes developing human beings and active citizens, not just skilled workers.

Putting the Movement Back into Civil Rights Teaching, edited by Deborah Menkart, Alana D. Murray, and Jenice L. View (Washington, DC: Teaching for Change and the Poverty and Race Research Action Council, 2004).

This book provides lessons and articles on how to go beyond a "heroes" approach to teaching about the Civil Rights Movement. It includes interactive and interdisciplinary lessons, readings, writings, photographs, illustrations, and interviews.

VOICES FROM THE CLASSROOM

"I STARTED OUT TEACHING in Chile. My first day teaching up here was like a punch in the face. All the silence and the straight lines — it spooked me. And I still haven't quite gotten over it. The effect is you have a whole lot of kids who really don't want to go to school. It's a battle I'm still fighting. You can't just diss straight lines and silence unless you have a viable alternative. And so that's where the struggle starts."

— Aron Corbett

Savage Inequalities: Children in America's Schools, by Jonathan Kozol (New York: Perennial, 1992).

This classic book about conditions in U.S. schools paints an unforgettable portrait of the underequipped, understaffed, and underfunded schools that are struggling to serve students in our inner cities and less-than affluent suburbs, and how U.S. schools systematically shortchange poor students and students of color.

The Skin That We Speak: Thoughts on Language and Culture in the Classroom, edited by Lisa Delpit and Joanne Kilgour Dowdy (New York: W. W. Norton, 2003).

WHERE TO FIND POSTERS, MAPS, AND OTHER RESOURCES

Maps to Help People Think, www.odt.org
ODT, Inc., P.O. Box 134, Amherst, MA 01004, 800-736-1293, email: odtstore@aol.com

Both the Peters Projection Map and the "What's Up? South!" world map challenge people to think differently about the world. The Peters Projection map accurately presents the area of all countries and explains how the commonly used Mercator projection distorts the sizes of continents, making Europe appear much larger than it is. The teaching guide *A New View of the World: Handbook to the Peters Projection World Map,* by Ward L. Kaiser, is also available here.

The National Women's History Project, www.nwhp.org
3343 Industrial Dr., Suite 4, Santa Rosa, CA 95403, 707-838-6000, fax: 707-838-0478, email: nwhp@aol.com

A nonprofit distributor of multicultural, women's history books, CDs, videos, posters, and curricula. The Learning Place page features teaching ideas and info at www.nwhp.org/tlp/main/main.html.

Northern Sun Merchandising, www2.northernsun.com
2916 E. Lake St., Minneapolis, MN 55406-2065, 800-258-8579, fax: 612-729-0149, email: nsm@scc.net

A distributor of valuable resources on environmental, gay/lesbian, multicultural, and feminist themes. Offers a particularly impressive collection of beautiful, classroom-friendly posters.

Thirteen essays by teachers offer fascinating and illuminating perspectives on the provocative issue of dialects in the classroom, a controversy sparked by the notorious Ebonics debate of the 1990s.

That's Not Fair!: A Teacher's Guide to Activism with Young Children, by Ann Pelo and Fran Davidson (St. Paul, MN: Redleaf Press, 2000).
Children have a natural sense of what's fair and what's not. This book helps teachers learn to use this characteristic to develop children's belief that they can change the world for the better. It includes real-life stories of activist children, combined with teachers' experiences and reflections. It also includes original songs for children and a resource list.

Through Indian Eyes: The Native Experience in Books for Children (Contemporary American Indian Issues, No. 7), edited by Beverly Slapin and Doris Seale (University of California: American Indian Studies Center, 1998).
Essays, poetry, an extensive bibliography, and critical reviews of children's books by and about Indian peoples. A dependable and honest guide for parents and instructors interested in teaching kids about the diversity of Native America.

Syracuse Cultural Workers, www.syrculturalworkers.com
P.O. Box 6367, Syracuse, NY 13217, 315-474-1132, fax (toll-free): 877-265-5399, email: scw@syrculturalworkers.com
A long-time distributor of multicultural and social-justice resources, including the Peace Calendar, which should adorn all classrooms.

Teaching for Change, www.teachingforchange.org
P.O. Box 73038, Washington, DC 20056-3038, 800-763-9131, fax: 202-238-0109, email: info@teachingforchange.org
Distributor and publisher of quality multicultural and social justice teaching materials, such as *Putting the Movement Back into Civil Rights Teaching* and *Beyond Heroes and Holidays* (for details see the above book list). This organization's catalog is the single best source for materials to help teachers to explore and teach about social justice issues.

— Bob Peterson

Turning on Learning: Five Approaches for Multicultural Teaching Plans for Race, Class, Gender, and Disability, by Carl A. Grant and Christine Sleeter (Saddle River, NJ: Prentice Hall, 1989).

A practical, hands-on guide to developing and delivering curriculum supporting multicultural education, with special attention to race, class, and gender issues.

What Keeps Teachers Going? by Sonia Nieto (New York: Teachers College Press, 2003).

In this deeply personal yet world-wise book, Nieto leads seven veteran Boston Public Schools teachers in reflecting on how they stay committed to teaching. The teachers speak movingly about the joys, frustrations, and rewards of teaching, and help articulate how and why good teachers remain committed to their work.

"Why Are All the Black Kids Sitting Together in the Cafeteria?" And Other Conversations About Race: A Psychologist Explains the Development of Racial Identity, by Beverly Daniel Tatum (New York: Basic Books, 1997).

An insightful exploration of the dynamics of race and racism in the United States. Tatum explores the process by which students explore and establish their racial identity, illuminates "why talking about racism is so hard" and suggests what we can do to make it easier. ∎

CHAPTER TWO

"What Am I Going to Teach?"

"Curriculum Is Everything That Happens"

AN INTERVIEW WITH VETERAN TEACHER RITA TENORIO

Rita Tenorio has spent more than 25 years teaching children in the early-elementary grades. Since 1988 she has taught at La Escuela Fratney, a public school in Milwaukee that she helped to found. Fratney features two-way bilingual education — all students learn in both English and Spanish — and a curriculum that emphasizes anti-racist, social justice education. In this interview by Leon Lynn, she offers encouragement and guidance to those just starting out in the teaching profession.

Do you think that the average person coming out of a teacher-education program in college is ready to be a teacher?

I would say this to them: You've spent a lot of time in school, you've had some experiences, you've been able to accumulate a lot of information, and lots of it is probably very, very good. But there are also a whole bunch of other things, important things, that you may not know yet. You need to be open to that and ready to learn things.

Like what?

Well, to begin with, if you haven't been around teachers who have a political consciousness, who have experience with the social and political effects of things that take place in the schools, you definitely have to learn about that. You can't be thinking that your classroom is a safe little place that's separated from the rest of the world. Schools are impacted by larger social forces, by the dynamics of who has power in our society, how decisions are made. These forces determine so many things, including whether schools are adequately funded, whether the students and their families are comfortable or struggling to make ends meet, so many things that affect what happens in the classroom.

I like to think that the people who have worked with us at Fratney have a sense of that, because we try to make it a real up-front issue. Fratney is built on the principles of anti-racism and multiculturalism, the idea that we're not just preparing students to take and pass tests, we're not just preparing them academically but also to play a conscious and active role in society, to recognize and combat racism, to actively pursue social justice. These are things that many new teachers may not have been exposed to.

What advice would you give to a new teacher who finds a job in a school where the students are from a culture the teacher doesn't know well?

I think all teachers, especially new teachers, have to work very hard at getting to know who their students are. I don't just mean what their favorite colors are, but understanding things about them and their families. When I was first teaching, I knew very little about African-American history and culture. My stereotypes were that the African-American children came from very poor families who didn't have much education, that they were city-bound kids. But then I began listening to the children, the stories they told, and I began to realize just how stereotyped and limited my understanding was. I remember hearing children talking about going camping with their families and realizing that I never would have imagined them doing that. That's just one small example.

How can the teacher start bridging those gaps?

It's the teacher's job to invite the students to bring that information into the classroom, to tell stories about their families, to feel valued for making that contribution and for who they are. And we need to make sure this applies to all the children, not just the cute and verbal ones who are acclimated to the culture of school. That tends to happen a lot: There's this picture in the teacher's mind of the ideal kid and this notion that things would be better "if you could just be more like so-and-so." And that's so limiting, so unfair.

Curriculum is everything that happens. It's not just books and lesson plans. It's relationships, attitudes, feelings, interactions. If kids feel safe, if they feel inspired, if they feel motivated, if they feel capable and successful, they're going to learn important and positive things. But if those elements are not there, if they feel disrespected or neglected in school, they're learning from that too. But they're not necessarily learning the curriculum you think you're teaching them.

Teachers are under ever-increasing pressure to "teach to the test," to drill everyone on the same narrow band of curriculum and keep test scores up. And in many places there is increased support for very strict, scripted curriculum and teaching, such as Direct Instruction. How can a teacher do the kinds of things you are saying are crucial, while coping with these pressures?

It's a paradox, to be sure. In school you learn all about multiple intelligences, and different ways and styles of learning, and then you start teaching and more often than not they hand you a curriculum

VOICES FROM THE CLASSROOM

"TEACHERS CAN BE AGENTS of change. We shouldn't accept the idea that we don't have the power to do anything in the situation. Even if you don't see yourself as a political person or someone with control over what you're doing, in reality, you're making thousands of political decisions every day. Not intervening when a student makes a racist comment is a political decision. Teaching from textbooks that emphasize only the European-American experience is another one. Those are political decisions that hurt students. You can also make choices that help students — choose to intervene when you hear a homophobic slur, choose to find books that represent the experiences of many different kinds of people, etc."

— Kelley Dawson Salas

and say, "This is how to do it." And you can't just walk away from that. But you have to try and find ways to go beyond what is being scripted. Maybe you have to follow a very narrow instructional model in

How can I start building community in my classroom?

Students spend the most of their waking hours in school, a place that can offer them both an education, in the broadest sense of the word, and a sense of belonging within a classroom community — something that can and should begin on their first school day.

Having a routine to follow in the beginning of the day helps students make the transition from home to school and feel secure. Greeting students at the classroom door, for example, can be a powerful way to communicate the message "I am glad you're here." It's also an opportunity to briefly check in with students: A lot could have happened since they left yesterday.

Another powerful routine is the class meeting, a scheduled time when students get to participate in a classwide discussion. This offers students the chance to share something of importance to them, as well as to practice active listening skills when others are sharing. It can also be a time when conflicts within the classroom can be addressed and collectively solved.

Pay attention to how students are seated. Small group seating — desks arranged in clusters instead of long rows — often helps build collaboration. To encourage students to make new friends, many teachers also find it helpful to periodically change the composition of these groups.

Classroom community also can emerge when students have the means to acknowledge transitions. For example, at the end of a unit of study, offer students time to reflect on what went well for them during the unit and challenges they encountered. Let them share their experiences and offer feedback to one another.

Never underestimate your role in helping to create a classroom community. By being honest and authentic with your students, the seeds of trust will be sown, and classroom community can grow and flourish.

— Dale Weiss

reading, for example, but maybe there are ways you can integrate a broader vision of reading into other subjects, like science or math. And there's another element: You have to be part of a culture that stands up and asks: "Is this the best thing for our children?" There are schools where those questions are never asked. It's up to teachers to play a role in changing that, in raising holy hell if necessary to advocate for the children.

How can a new teacher, new in the building and district, do that?

It may seem overwhelming for people who are newer in the profession, but in some ways I think it's actually easier for them. I know I had a lot more energy for this stuff when I was younger and didn't have children of my own at home to care for. When you're young and new, you can establish who you are and what your priorities are.

One thing that really helped me was getting together with a network of people, searching out people who felt the way I did, and staying connected with them. You want to find the people in your own building whom you feel you can communicate with, whom you can raise questions with. You want to start looking in your district: I found some terrific people in the teacher union and through some professional development activities. There are networks and groups that stretch all across the country that address some of these issues, like multiculturalism, and you can tap into those. If you have friends from the university, and other people you've known for a while, you stay connected with them. Find people in the community, people who aren't teachers, who are interested in education issues. Get on the web and start hunting for good websites and listservs. Then it's not just your voice out there in the wilderness. And together you can make good things happen. ■

"How Am I Going to Do This?"

GUIDELINES FOR DEVELOPING CURRICULUM

Each of us has experienced the excitement and trepidation of taking everything we have learned in college and teacher-training programs and trying to apply it in a real, live classroom.

It is no easy task translating the goals and ideals that brought us to teaching into our daily practice. And each of us has had moments in our early days when we have felt less than prepared and less than successful, and asked ourselves: "How am I going to do this?"

Contrary to what some off-the-shelf curriculum packages try to tell you, there is no one-size-fits-all formula that can tell teachers what to teach their students and how to teach it. Each grade level, each school, each classroom of kids has its own dynamics.

But we think there are some basic ideas and concepts that new teachers should keep in mind as they get started on their careers:

Don't underestimate what you bring to teaching. While it's true that new teachers have a lot to learn, they also have valuable insight into the needs of students, because they were students themselves not long ago. And because they are just beginning their careers, new teachers are often very self-reflective, and willing to consciously analyze their practice. They are still thinking in very literal terms about how to connect with kids and communicate effectively with

BY
THE
EDITORS

them. Hold on to your memories of being a student. Reflect often on what it means to teach with a social justice perspective. Use the excitement and energy you bring to your new career to make a difference in the lives of the students you teach.

Cut yourself some slack. Nobody gets this teaching thing exactly right at the beginning. There will be days when nothing goes the way you planned. Guess what? Experienced teachers have days like that too. Part of being a teacher is learning the lessons those days offer, dealing with difficulties as they crop up and taking the fullest advantage of your successes, constantly examining your practice and trying to improve it. One of the best things about this job is being able to start fresh each day. In both a literal and figurative sense, "erase the board" after those hard, hard days and start with a "clean slate" the next.

...But don't let yourself get lazy. There's a difference between giving yourself a break and giving yourself an excuse. If you give in to the cynicism that says some kids "are just too hard to teach," or if you just teach straight out of the textbook all day without critically examining what you are doing, you are selling yourself and your students short. Then your classroom becomes another place where the inequities of society are reproduced, instead of a place where students get the tools they need to make the world a better place. Prepare yourself to work long and hard. This is a difficult, yet challenging, exhausting, yet rewarding job. It's never boring and it's so worth it.

Build community. It cannot be said too often that the hours invested in developing your classroom community are the ones that pay off most. These activities and projects are the ones that give you the insights you need to connect with your students and build the trust necessary to explore deeper issues with them. Here is the place to work at "leveling the playing field" in your classroom, to make students' experiences with you safe and fair regardless of their cultural background or level of academic achievement. This is also where you can give them responsibility and the experience of learning the roles of friend, citizen, advocate, and leader.

Teach everybody. Part of building community is learning about everyone who is there. Use exercises and activities that get everyone involved. Students should not only receive an invitation to participate, but they should know that they are expected to become part of the group. This is never an easy task, especially with children who are accustomed to sitting out, who may be very hesitant or resistant to becoming involved. Don't just cherry-pick the answers from kids who already are willing to give them. It has to be about everyone doing high-quality work, not just some. That expectation should be clear from the beginning.

Be consistent. Establish routines and procedures with the kids early on in the year. Let them know your expectations about behavior and stick to them. Work with your colleagues to maintain these standards as they move throughout the school: to the lunch room, to the

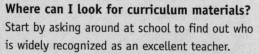

Where can I look for curriculum materials?
Start by asking around at school to find out who is widely recognized as an excellent teacher. Some teachers will be on almost everyone's list. Call or email these teachers and ask if there would be a convenient time for you to come by and talk curriculum and raid their files. Make sure you go to their classrooms so that they'll have materials handy. It's fine to get "greatest hit" lesson plans, but it's more useful to have an experienced teacher walk you through a full unit. Ask that teacher who else you should talk with, and whether or not there are networks of social justice teachers in the area.

The best place to find published social justice teaching materials is the Teaching for Change catalog, available at www.teachingforchange.org or 800-763-9131. The print version of this catalog is revised twice yearly, and the online version is updated regularly.

Rethinking Schools also offers a collection of social justice teaching materials and maintains a critical-teaching listserv open to all *Rethinking Schools* subscribers. Check out both of these at www.rethinkingschools.org. Join the listserv and ask about everything from ideas for teaching the U.S. Constitution to a good source for posters for your classroom.

Also check out the Syracuse Cultural Workers catalog at www.syrculturalworkers.com.

— Bill Bigelow

music room, to the gym. You have to be consistent. Kids can't think that it's OK to be well-behaved in your classroom and wild in the hallway or with other staff. And remember: How you interact with people in the building reflects your belief in the values that guide your work with them. How do you relate to your colleagues? To parents? When you walk down the hall, do you make eye contact or stare at the floor? Students notice these things. And they mirror what they see in us.

Move beyond the textbook. Many teachers, especially new teachers, fall into the trap of teaching straight out of an assigned textbook all the time. You may feel you need to use the textbook — especially if your principal makes it clear you're expected to. And even when we have more freedom to develop curriculum, many of us feel unprepared for that challenge when we are just starting our careers. Go ahead and use the book if you need to, but use it critically. Ask yourself and your students: What are the implicit values being presented by this textbook? Whose voices are being heard? Whose voices are absent? Does your textbook, for example, say Columbus discovered America, without bothering to tell the stories of the people who were already there and who were brutally exploited by Columbus and his crew? Introduce supplemental materials to round out the worldview presented in the text. Stepping beyond the limits of the textbook and learning to critically examine texts are valuable skills for students and teachers alike.

Don't try to go it alone. Teaching can be a very isolating experience, but it doesn't have to be. Find others with whom you can talk, vent, reflect. Hook into a network of people who are thinking about the issues you are working on. Ask yourself who can help: Colleagues in the building? College friends? Your union? Staff in other schools? Are there ways to seek out like-minded teachers on the Internet? There are many good books and resources to help you think critically about your teaching: We have provided some places to start in the lists that begin on pages 66 and 70. Many of us would have never survived without the help and encouragement of our families, friends, and colleagues, and the support provided by networks and associations that offer help to new teachers. Don't be afraid to ask for that support.

Assume nothing ... and keep an open mind. You won't know immediately what your students know and don't know. Don't assume, for example, that your fifth graders have already gotten experience or practice working in cooperative groups. In the same vein, don't assume that kids with Hispanic surnames speak Spanish, or that the students of color come from impoverished or illiterate families. Don't make judgments about what you don't know. Inform yourself. Communicate with families, learn about the community. Talk to the teachers in the earlier grades. Listen, but be cautious of their advice. Then be prepared to teach the kids the basic skills and processes they'll need in your class. And remember, while you may have to cover

My students don't bring back their homework. Should I keep assigning it?

First ask yourself some questions: Why are you giving homework? Is there a school policy, or is it up to the teacher? In many places it is a timeworn tradition that students have homework, or it may be that parents demand it or have banned it.

What is the purpose served by homework? Is it a real opportunity for students to review or practice a skill? Is it meant to let families know what is going on in class? Or is it just "busy work"? What happens to the work that students bring back? Who looks at it? How is it used or not used?

These questions are just the beginning.

If you really want your students to take homework seriously, spend time on it and return it. Be sure the content is meaningful and connected to their lives, the classroom, or both.

Homework has to be thought through and planned like any other part of the curriculum. Involve students in the development and use of the information in their homework. Let them know that you and they will need the data they collected, or the words of the person they interviewed, to continue the work in the classroom during the coming days.

Homework can be an opportunity to learn about the lives and perspectives of students and their families. It can be a chance for kids to practice collecting data, to experiment with materials and ideas, to gain expertise in conducting surveys and interviewing others. Asking for the knowledge, ideas, and per-the basics, like writing a sentence, that doesn't mean you're stuck writing boring sentences.

Encourage kids to bring their lives into the classroom. Academic skills and strategies can be taught while using the experiences and insights of students as the basis for activities and projects. Encourage the acceptance of multiple perspectives on a topic: Allow opportunities for different ideas to emerge. Teachers cannot be not totally non-judgmental here. You can't let students argue for viewpoints that are wrong or misinformed. But there's a difference between fuzzing up the facts and being open to alternate interpretations. Try saying less of "that's wrong," and more of "I never thought of that before," as a way of exploring ideas. Don't shut down kids for seeing things differently, or teach them to expect that conforming is the only way to get a good grade.

---

spectives of students and their families will give you and your students the rich beginnings of many classroom conversations.

You also have to be sensitive to the circumstances students face outside of school. Is there a place for the student to do work at home? Will there be another person available to help with the work or to see that it's done? What resources does your student have outside of school? Does the family have access to computers or other technology, for example? Don't assume that all your students do or do not have resources. Ask.

If you have students who can't or don't do homework, you can also find ways for them to complete the work at school. **Here are some examples of homework assignments that invite students' lives into the classroom.**

Interview someone in your family about:

An upcoming holiday, a current event, experiences that they may have had.

Respond to the question:

What is peace? What is justice? What is your best advice to me? What do you know about _____?

— Rita Tenorio

Keep it real. Content that connects to kids' experiences will help motivate them and you. Let them know that their lives are welcome, their input is valued.

Don't settle for the status quo. Instead, what will move the kids to a place where they will become more thoughtful?

I hate the textbook I've been given to use. What can I do?

In order to present students with multiple perspectives on any topic, it is likely that you will need more than one resource. Part of the challenge in becoming a social justice teacher is finding the materials you will need to supplement the books you have available in your school. Then there is also the trick of finding the time and opportunities in the weekly schedule to use them. It is not easy, but it is worth the energy you expend.

Take the time to review the textbooks you're given, then determine where you will need to add on to what you've got. Start with your school library. Tap the public library as well, for classroom literature. If you have access to a university, see if it has collections of curriculum materials available for lending. Then get on the Internet: Start with the resources and web links you'll find at www.rethinkingschools.org.

Monthly book clubs like Scholastic or Troll often offer quality literature at a great price. They are an inexpensive way to begin collecting multiple copies of books for use in reading instruction. Don't be afraid to ask if there is money in the school budget to add to your classroom collection.

Songs and poetry are great sources of alternative perspectives too. And you can use data and information from the news to help students explore concepts in math, science, and other curricular areas.

If you still feel you're "stuck" with poor resources, remember that you have the ability to help your students look critically at what they are reading and see the shortcomings for them-

Let students see you as a person. Ask yourself: What will kids remember about me? Your students need to see you as a human being. Don't be afraid to open up some, to share your life a little. Let the kids hear about your outside interests — music, sports, membership at the Y, family activities. Let them see you involved in the community, your interest in politics, your concern for the neighborhood. If they see you connected to things beyond the classroom, that humanizes you.

Take care of yourself. The students you teach need you to be there for them every day. Yes, you have to spend long hours of work preparing, organizing, doing and redoing plans for the lessons you

---

selves. Help them find ways to "talk back" to the textbook and teach them how to find other perspectives that are not represented in its pages.

— Rita Tenorio

If your principal has told you to use the textbook, defying a direct order from him/her will generally be considered insubordination and will land you in trouble, or even the unemployment line. However, perhaps there are other people in your school or department who don't like this book. Ask around to find out. Get together with those people. Write up a critique of the book and propose alternative curriculum.

In the short term, go ahead and use the book but use it critically. Invite students to read between the lines: Whose perspectives are missing? Was America "discovered" or "invaded"? See "Students as Textbook Detectives" in *Rethinking Our Classrooms, Volume 1,* or *Rethinking Columbus* for lots of ideas on how to engage students in a critique of their textbooks. (See pages 67 and 68 for details.)

In a nutshell: If you feel like you have to use the assigned text, use it, but find other materials as well. Even if you "use" the textbook, any good administrator will expect you to supplement it with lots of other materials.

— Bill Bigelow

will teach. *But* you will be no good to them if you are not healthy, both physically and emotionally. Find the balance you need to be most effective. And relax on your time off: It will make you a better teacher.

Put anti-racism and multiculturalism at the heart of your work. These concepts should be at the core of what you do each day. Model for your students how an adult translates these ideas into real-world practice. Live a life dedicated to social justice, and the students will see that in you. ∎

Q/A

How can I help my students stay organized?
Organization is a skill that's learned. That means we must plan for it, just as we plan to teach a lesson on rhyming words or writing persuasive paragraphs.

First, I wrote into our daily schedule "clean desks" about every two weeks, so that my students were prepared for it, just like any other activity during the day.

I explained why we did this: It made it easier for them to keep their work neat and find it easily. Then our days moved more smoothly: We didn't have to stop because half of us couldn't find our math folders or journals.

Students kept a homework folder, an assignment book, and a journal in their desks. Other than their textbooks, a pencil, and a 24-count box of crayons, that was it. The less there was in the desks, the less chance there was for clutter to take root.

Next, we went through the cleaning process step by step: Remove all texts and put them in a pile. Remove all loose papers, file the ones you need to keep and and recycle the ones you don't. And so on.

Finally, I practiced what I preached: I forced myself to clean my desk and I shared with my kids that I had done so. Afterall, how could I expect them to listen to me if my desk was a complete mess?

— Stephanie Walters

Dealing with Standardized Tests

I began teaching elementary school in 1999, and since then there has not yet been a single year when my school did not require me to do some amount of "test prep" to get my students ready to take standardized tests.

It's a fact of life in today's schools: Kids have to take standardized tests and teachers are expected to prepare them. Federal legislation makes sure that schools whose students do poorly on tests face strict consequences: Parents must be informed that they can transfer to a different school, funds may be taken away, administrators and staff can be replaced. Fear of being punished drives many schools to place a high priority on helping students score well on tests.

But, you may ask, what's wrong with wanting our students to score well on tests? For most of us, it only makes sense that if we are going to ask our students to do something, we want to help them be as successful at it as possible.

BY
KELLEY
DAWSON
SALAS
There are lots of potential problems with standardized tests and with the activities we use to get students ready for them. If not kept in check, a narrow, obsessive focus on standardized tests can dumb down the curriculum and make school a boring, lifeless place for both students and

teachers. I've learned that this can happen even in a school where educators are committed to rigorous, child-centered curriculum and opposed to excessive standardized testing. I have found that even though it's difficult, I have to speak up when my colleagues and administrators discuss testing. Otherwise, testing and test prep activities can eat up a large part of the school year and leave little time for real teaching and learning.

Here's how that happened one year in my classroom.

A School "In Need of Improvement"

In September, I learned that my school was on the "schools in need of improvement" list. The test was coming in November, and we needed to get the kids ready fast, so they could do well on the test and we could get off the list. We immediately undertook a drastic change in our fourth-grade program (the grade I teach and the most heavily tested grade in my school). We scrapped what we were doing in reading and math, recruited every additional support staff person available, and began to provide small group test-prep activities in math and reading for two hours a day.

To make room for test prep, we put the district's own math curriculum on hold for two months: Instead we needed to teach an

---

Q/A

Should I leave the school I'm in?
You have to make an assessment of whether or not you can survive at the school you've landed in. Is there a fundamental mismatch with your values in terms of pedagogical approach? And if there is, can you struggle to change things within your school? Are there enough allies to do that? Or do you have to find a new school? Maybe you can find a new setting and move in and be comfortable because it's already established, or you can do what some of us did and create a whole new public school like when we started La Escuela Fratney in Milwaukee. However, I would not underestimate how hard it is to create your own school.

— Bob Peterson

"overview" of all the concepts that would be on the test. We stopped teaching reading as a subject that integrated content in science and social studies, because we needed to group our students across classrooms, strictly by reading level, to help them make the most progress possible before the test.

Hands-on activities and science and social studies content had no place in this test-prep program. There was very little time left each day once the test prep groups were done, and we had to cut back on the activities that we normally do in the fall, including our study of water quality in the Milwaukee River and our beach cleanup at Lake Michigan.

During the entire fall of that school year, I came to work each day infuriated and demoralized, and went home each night feeling even worse. I hated wasting class time on test prep. I hated feeling like we were racing the clock, cramming as much information as possible into 9-year-old brains before the day of the test.

I resented the fact that I had to participate in all of this simply because I was a fourth-grade teacher. I was angry that I had only had a small voice in the process by which our entire curriculum was hastily revised and our school year was derailed. I felt that our school administrators had made decisions under pressure. I felt trapped because I didn't agree with those decisions, and yet I was the person that had to carry them out. I thought about transferring to a different grade and even about leaving teaching all together.

I also felt an overwhelming responsibility to my students, especially those who were learning English as a second language. This was the first year they were required to take their tests in English, and on top of everything else, teachers had been instructed to make whatever accommodations they needed, so the test would be as reliable a measure as possible of their academic knowledge. This amounted to translating the test into Spanish, allowing extra time, and spending lots of time reminding students that they are intelligent even though taking a test in their second language might make them doubt that. I thought the system was horribly unfair for second language learners, and I felt like it was my responsibility to protect them from this unfairness.

We started the testing process in November. It lasted eight school days — almost two entire weeks. By the time Thanksgiving rolled around, the test was over, and on December 1, we were ready to start what we considered our "real school year."

The million-dollar question: Did it work? Well ... we got off the list, but not exactly because of our scores that particular year. While we had been busy doing test prep, our school had filed an appeal based on data from the previous year, and we succeeded in having the "schools in need of improvement" label removed.

A Different Approach

During those three months (nearly a third of the school year), many of my colleagues and I came to the conclusion that the test-prep activities took up too much classroom time and that some of them were not helpful. We met. We debated. And in the end we decided to take a different approach the following year — one that was far less intrusive into the life of our classroom and, happily, one that allowed us to return to our normal math and science curriculum.

We decided to teach reading as we normally would, but to include a few multiple-choice, "practice-test" type activities, and with some instruction on how to do those kinds of test activities successfully. And we decided that trying to cover a year's worth of math curriculum in two months is just not possible. We went back to using the district's curriculum and pacing schedule but added a strong focus at the beginning of the year on how to solve word problems and how to explain mathematical solutions — something important to getting good test scores, but also something we definitely want our kids to know how to do regardless.

Through these experiences I learned that striking a balance is key. I know that I cannot ignore the tests or the need to prepare my students for them. I know I need to do some things to familiarize my students with the test format and the types of questions they will encounter. I also think it's reasonable to have students experience a simulated testing environment prior to the actual test: Practice runs will help cut down on nervousness when the real testing starts.

What I am not willing to do is to spend every day of the year using multiple-choice, worksheet-type activities simply because "that's what they'll see on the test."

Every school is different and there is no magic formula for how much test prep to do or how to do it. What is crucial is that teachers and administrators talk with each other about the testing that occurs at each grade level and that they agree on a plan that prepares students sufficiently without overtaking the entire curriculum.

The staff at my school discusses testing often. As a new teacher, I sometimes find it difficult to stand up for what I believe. Even though many of my colleagues are philosophically opposed to the testing craze, there is nonetheless an enormous amount of pressure to demonstrate academic proficiency and sufficient "adequate yearly

---

FOR FURTHER INFORMATION

FairTest: The National Center for Fair & Open Testing,
www.fairtest.org

FairTest provides information, technical assistance, and advocacy on a broad range of testing concerns, and works to end the misuse of standardized tests and to promote responsible alternatives. The website offers fact sheets, links to more comprehensive resources, and information about the *Examiner,* the group's newsletter.

Susan Ohanian Speaks Out, www.susanohanian.org

Ohanian, a prominent and well-respected researcher, uses this website to dispense news and information on the standardized testing craze. Her presentation is often entertaining, as when she presents her "Outrage of the Day" or warns that you could take all the sincerity among standardized testing advocates, "place it in the navel of a fruit fly and still have room for three caraway seeds and the heart of a member of the Business Roundtable." But the information she collects on testing is serious, deep, and a real boon to teachers seeking alternatives to fill-in-the-blank assessment.

Failing Our Kids: Why The Testing Craze Won't Fix Our Schools, edited by Barbara Miner and Kathy Swope (Rethinking Schools, 2000). www.rethinkingschools.org

More than 50 articles and reports from teachers, parents, students, and researchers offer a compelling critique of standardized tests, as well as a wealth of practical information on better ways to assess how children are learning. The Rethinking Schools website offers detailed information from the book, downloadable samples, and online purchasing information.

progress," and that can lead to all sorts of curriculum changes that aren't necessarily good for kids.

As teachers, we must advocate for our students and insist upon their right to real, rigorous curriculum. If we don't stand our ground, we run the risk of allowing our curriculum to wither away into endless and meaningless worksheets and practice tests — which won't keep kids engaged in learning, and won't keep good teachers engaged in teaching!

In Wisconsin, for example, teachers, parents, and community activists formed the Coalition for Responsible Assessment to advocate for curbs on the use of standardized tests and to link issues of testing to broader issues about the quality of education available in public schools. This coalition has given teachers a way to connect with their peers, as well as a broader spectrum of the community, around issues of testing and teaching.

As a new teacher, it can be hard to decide when to stand up and advocate for something and when to close your door and quietly teach the things you believe will engage children and help them learn. It is worth the effort, though, to craft an approach for dealing with testing and test prep that works for you at your particular school. Hopefully, such an approach can allow you the opportunity to teach a rigorous, interesting, high-quality curriculum for many years to come. ■

Reading
Between the Bubbles

TEACHING STUDENTS TO
CRITICALLY EXAMINE TESTS

Tests today are high-stakes. Based on test scores, students are retained, placed in summer school and remedial classes; schools are reconstituted or otherwise penalized; and in some instances, teachers' and principals' salaries rise and fall. Students, especially those who fail the tests, may internalize the failure, and question their ability and their intelligence. They learn to blame themselves, and some come to believe they will not succeed because they are not capable enough.

As my daughter said after receiving a 3 ("not competent") on an oral Spanish test one year, "Maybe I don't have what it takes." The test took away the experience of animated conversations with her host family in Cuernavaca, as well as her ability to navigate Mexico City. Instead of questioning the validity of the measurement tool as an "authentic assessment," especially compared to her experience in Mexico, she questioned herself.

My friends at low-achieving elementary schools have been counseled to redesign their regular curricula so that students can get accustomed to multiple-choice questions. But in a classroom where we try to develop students' capacity to think critically and imaginatively, that's not easy. How can a role play about an

BY
LINDA
CHRISTENSEN

important historical or social issue be reformatted into a multiple-choice activity? How does an A-B-C-D answer format encourage students to imagine themselves as an interned Japanese American or a Cherokee Indian facing government-ordered removal?

Teachers are also asked to mimic the more "authentic" assessments in fairly inauthentic ways. A kindergarten colleague, for example, was asked by the third-grade teachers to prepare students for the state's six-trait analysis scoring guide by giving them scores of 1 to 6 on everything from lining up at the door to tying their shoes and counting.

Clearly, this isn't the kind of teaching we want in our classrooms. To achieve real gains in knowledge and skills, students need a rich curriculum with varied opportunities to use their learning in real world activities. This material will generate growth that may or may not be reflected in test scores, but will increase the likelihood of students seeing themselves as readers, writers, historians, scientists, mathematicians, and thinkers.

However, I live in Oregon, a state that has filled our classrooms with tests. As a teacher and mother who has patched up the wounds test scores have left behind, and as a victim of a school that was reconstituted in part due to low test scores, I am a firm advocate in fighting against the over-assessment of students. But I also believe we must create an opportunity to teach students to critique the tests as we coach them on how to increase their performance.

Examining the Origins and Purpose of Tests

We may have contempt for the tests, but learning how to take them is a survival skill in today's society. Thus, I want to support and even deepen students' critiques of the tests, but in a way that equips them to succeed on the tests. The question for new and veteran teachers alike is: How do we establish a critical stance on assessments while preparing students to be successful on them? How can we prepare students to take tests and at the same time equip students to be critical of them?

One of my most important aims as a teacher is to encourage my students to think critically about aspects of life that they might otherwise simply take for granted. Unfortunately, testing is a piece of school life that students accept as part of their education. From the time they are in third grade in Oregon, students sit through batteries of tests. Their scores are sent home, informing their parents where they stand in the education pecking order of other third graders in the district.

Students come to expect that, like beef, they will receive a ranking from the government: exceeds, meets, conditionally meets, does not meet. They move through school dragging these test scores behind them. If I don't interrupt this routine, I allow students to internalize the state's labels. Students, particularly students whose test scores lag behind, may accept placement in non-college track courses, and otherwise lower their expectations. Counselors won't recommend them for the higher-level math and science classes needed for acceptance into a four-year university. Of course, some students break out of the rut test scores have carved for them. But for many, their scores mark their place, not only in school, but in life after school.

One way to prevent this internalization is to take the time to critically examine the origins of the testing movement and the tests themselves, to get students to honestly appraise their own abilities instead of accepting the judgment of the exams, and to help them develop an interior monologue that talks back to the labels.

In my classes, I begin by tackling the tests with students, and then teaching them to create new ones. While my junior and senior students at Portland's Jefferson High School weren't saddled with the reading, writing, and math tests that Oregon third, fifth, eighth, and tenth graders currently take, my students had their behinds kicked by the SATs. After their encounters with these grueling tests, they fumed at me and their math teachers. "Those tests might as well have been written in Greek!" Shameka said after her Saturday was ruined by the exams. For my students, an investigation of the history of the SATs was as critical as teaching them how to improve their scores.

To help students understand the origins of the exam and help them put their scores in perspective, my class read the chapter "The Cult of Mental Measurement" from David Owen's book *None of the Above*. Students were shocked by what they discovered about the founder of the SATs, Carl Campbell Brigham: According to Owen, he published in the same eugenics journal as Adolph Hitler and was convinced that there should be stronger immigration laws to protect the "contamination of the American intellect" by "Catholics, Greeks, Hungarians, Italians, Jews, Poles, Russians, Turks, and — especially — Negroes."

But even without this gem of a chapter, getting students to investigate the origins and uses of tests in their school district or state is a good place to start. (See Bill Bigelow's "Testing, Tracking, and Toeing the Line: A Role Play on the Origins of the Modern High School," in

Rethinking Our Classrooms, Volume 1, to help students develop a critique of the historical motivation behind the testing industry.)

Many teachers may choose not to take on an in-class study of tests, but even then it's important for us as teachers to familiarize ourselves with this history, so that we can talk with students when they encounter the tests.

Examining the Tests

Once students cast a critical eye on the origins of the tests, I help them improve their performance by examining both the content and the format of the tests themselves. The more they know about how the questions are put together, as well as the vocabulary of the material, the better prepared they are to meet the challenge.

In my sophomore Language Arts class at Grant High School in Portland, students demystified the state tests and used their knowledge to teach others about their discoveries. We examined practice reading tests that I downloaded from the Oregon Department of Education's website. We looked at the instructions and the content. We looked at the test's text passages and asked: "Whose background knowledge is honored here? Whose culture is represented? Whose culture and knowledge is missing? How would that make a difference in test results?"

Most of my sophomores agreed with their classmate Greg's critique of the test's reliance on short, random passages: "I thought the stories would be things we could relate to. We drift off when they don't interest us. They are disconnected. We'd be more likely to stick with it if we cared about what we read." They were quick to note that this test did not really measure their ability to read — which for them meant reading novels and short stories. As Greg so aptly described, tests are disconnected short passages followed by five or six questions. Students may have defined "reading" too narrowly, but they grasped an essential point neglected by the test makers: Reading is sustained and cumulative. Our understanding of the text builds over time.

My students also pointed out that the tests had more items about rural life than about urban life. Test selections included a snippet from Mark Twain about mosquitoes, a piece by Gary Paulsen about sled dogs in Alaska, and a Barry Lopez essay about wolves' howls. They also included a legal index, a chart about global gold production, and a calendar of upcoming events in Alaska. Students didn't find any of these particularly interesting or useful. Mostly, they were puzzled by the selections: Why these and not others? Students discussed how when they got bored and lost focus, they stopped taking the test seriously. Some reported bubbling in the rest of the test without reading the items; others just quit. A few students at Jefferson, who sensed the test's disrespect for African-American experience by omission, simply bubbled obscenities on the answer sheets.

This is important information for me as teacher. The value of the test scores — which I have doubts about to begin with — becomes negligible. Students' discussion also helps illuminate the huge discrepancy between their past test scores and their abilities. While some might attribute the students' refusal to mere laziness, I understand that, in part, it's a form of survival: They need to be able to say "I didn't try" if they receive a low test score. But resisting these tests can sabotage their own futures.

Developing Test-Taking Strategies

After students discuss their reactions to the content of several tests, they practice taking one of the sample tests. When they complete the exercise, I divide them into small groups and ask them to share their answers to the test questions and discuss what evidence from the reading informed their choices. I want them to understand that although they might disagree about the answers and the questions might be poorly worded, they have a better chance of getting more answers "correct" if they go back to the text to find support for their choice.

I also let them know that I have given the test to a number of teachers, and that they disagreed on some of the answers. In other words, the test answers are not perfect and even good readers come up with conflicting answers. During this activity, students also share their strategies — if they used any — for taking the sample test.

Then I give students the "correct" answers, according to the Oregon Department of Education (ODE), and I ask them to note in the margin the type of question, based on ODE's Reading and Literature Content Standards: word meaning, locating information, literal comprehension, inferential comprehension, evaluative comprehension, literary forms, or literary elements and devices. I do this for two reasons: I want students to understand the types of questions they will be asked, and I also want to poke holes in the questions themselves.

Students put up a fuss about the state's categories. "That's not a literary form!" one student fumed after I told them that's how the state had classified a legal index. The point of this activity is for students to understand that the questions vary based on the reading and literature content standard the test is attempting to cover, and sometimes the state's labels are confusing. I want students to cut the tests down to size, to know that the tests are not infallible; that humans, not gods, make them.

Then I ask students to note if they missed a certain kind of question more often — locating information versus literary elements, for example — because it does indicate the kinds of strategies individual students need to use. Word meaning questions, for example, often involve using context clues. And missing literary forms most often means that a student needs to brush up on that category.

We also discuss and create a class list of the strategies to use on the test. After our final round of working with the tests, students in my sophomore class at Grant came up with the following list:

- Read question first.
- Locate key words in question.
- Note type of question:
  In passage — word meaning, graph.
  Throughout passage — inference based on gathering clues.
  Not in passage — your conclusion based on evidence in passage.
- Be a detective — look for clues.
- Use the process of elimination.
- 50/50 — guess when you can eliminate two choices.

By engaging in this process, students learn to critique the tests, but also how to maneuver within them.

Once students have the basic format down, I give them a test I construct using high-interest material. I have used "Doin' the Louvre" from master slam poet Patricia Smith as well as poems by Jimmy Santiago Baca and Martín Espada. I collect articles by and about teens in the *Oregonian* and in magazines — "Eggs and Twinkies," about race in the Asian community, or "I Love Skratching," a critique of a Gap ad. I follow the test question format from the state, using their categories — word meaning, inferential comprehension, literary elements, and the like.

When I give students my test, I also pass out highlighters and ask them to read with a highlighter in hand. We discuss what to highlight based on our previous discussions: key words in the questions, for example, and key sections of the passage that correspond to the question. After students take my test, we once again scrutinize the types of questions and refine their strategies.

Creating Tests: Thinking Like a Test Maker

Then I turn students loose to create their own tests in small groups. Each group has to create a test using the kinds of items typically found in the Oregon tests: a poem, a graph, a passage from a short story or essay. Then they create questions, typically five, to go with their passage. Afterwards I find the best models, copy their tests, and students once again practice their test-taking skills.

When students think like a test maker, certainly their ability to read the test is enhanced, but something else happens as well: They realize that these are just questions about a reading. There is nothing magical, nothing omnipotent about them, nothing that marks these as the questions one must answer in order to be "smart." In other words, this process helps demystify the power of the test makers.

The work I've described here may raise student scores by a few points, and help students question the legitimacy of the tests as well as their results. But teaching students to examine the history and motives of local and state tests, and preparing them for the big day(s), is no substitute for fighting to end the encroachment of assessments in our classrooms. As teachers and parents we can organize against the broader attack on public education that allows fill-in-the-bubble tests to dominate our classrooms, and makes students question their abilities. ∎

References

None of the Above: The Truth Behind the SATs, by David Owen with Marilyn Doerr (Lanham, MD: Rowman & Littlefield, 1999).

Rethinking Our Classrooms, Volume 1 (Milwaukee: Rethinking Schools, 1994). See page 67 for more information.

Creating a Literate and Passionate Community

I knew that after the last week of classes in Period 3, English 10, I would never see some of my students again. Michael was leaving to live with his mom in Milwaukee; D.J. might be moving back to Chicago and might be taking classes at an area technical college; Janet was opting to leave "regular" high school classes for a work-to-learn program.

Teaching is a strange way to mark the passing of time: Students arrive at the same time every day and, together, we figure each other out. Throughout the year, I felt these students becoming a physical part of my identity.

In my first year of teaching, I felt my chest condensing with blows from the administration, other teachers, and policies that I could not control. I survived a twitch under my right eye, stress-induced hives, and endless nights of grading and writing lessons while having to stretch funds to cover my student loans. I felt guilty for not spending enough time with my partner, not doing my writing, and having to go to bed at nine o'clock.

BY TRACY WAGNER

But I also felt my heart widening with more anger and love and concern than I have ever felt before. At the end, I found myself wondering: What will happen when these students are gone?

While I had enjoyed a spectrum of emotions in all of my English classes during my first year of teaching, my Period 3 class was the hardest for me to let go. Within my high school's tracking system, this class rested at the "regular" level — under the TAG (Talented and Gifted) and ACAMO (Academically Motivated) tracks, but above self-contained special education. The students in that class were an array of ethnicities; all came from middle-class to lower-income homes, and some were labeled as "at-risk." Many students received special education services.

"Remember Me"

On the last day of class, as the students chatted, I laid my own poem on one of the desks in the circle. Earlier in the week, armed with the "Remember Me" lesson plan from Linda Christensen's *Reading, Writing, and Rising Up: Teaching About Social Justice and the Power of the Written Word* (see page 68), I had placed students' names and mine in a hat. After choosing a name, students were to write a poem, praising what they remembered about this person in our class. The word had spread fast — not a small feat in a large urban school — and students had been able to explain the lesson before I even opened my mouth.

VOICES FROM THE CLASSROOM

"START TEACHING BEFORE you actually get a job. Begin putting your curriculum together. Decide what subjects or grade levels you'll most likely be teaching — even if you haven't yet been hired — and begin to prepare. With every article you read, think about how to turn it into a lesson, how to bring a particular concept to life for students. Meet with more experienced teachers, raid their files, and build your own before you get a job."

— Bill Bigelow

I wondered if the poems would live up to my expectations. I wanted them to be gifts, something that the recipients could take to remember our classroom community and their place in it. As I helped students brainstorm, a small part of me feared that I had not created the community that I had worked for since day one. Listening to their questions — "What if I got the name of someone I don't like?" "What if I've never talked to this person?" "What if there's really nothing good to say? — I thought back on the year's activities and wondered if I had been overly optimistic.

Connecting Students and the World

Throughout the year, I had designed, collaborated on, and discovered hands-on units that use literature to help students explore their lives and connect to the larger community and world. I wanted students to become more "literate," which, to me, meant not only working on basic reading and writing skills, but becoming compassionate members of society, capable of being agents of change. With this in mind, I started the year with a poetry unit inspired by Janice Mirikitani's poem "Who Is Singing This Song?" Mirikitani explains the need to honor our ancestors' work by changing the injustices of the present.

How do I get started planning a teaching unit?

Often a unit begins with a central piece of literature or history. I examine the piece to uncover what lens, what approach, I will take with the material. I construct a question that I want students to answer by reading, writing, and discussing from the central text as well as a variety of other texts — movies, poetry, first-person narratives — including their own lives. For example, when I teach Alice Walker's *The Color Purple,* we ask about the roles of men and women in society. We read the novel, but we also look at images of women and men in advertising. We read "Jury of Her Peers" and "The Yellow Wallpaper," and poems by Sharon Olds, Ethelbert Miller, and Anne Sexton. We watch *Defending Our Lives,* a documentary about abused women who are in prison for killing their abusers. We interview men and women in our lives.

At other times, the question is the central focus of the unit, and I find a variety of texts with diverse voices to answer it — again including the students' voices. For example, in my unit on the politics of language, I begin with the question, "Is

She writes: "Who is singing this song?/I am./pulled by hands of history not to sit/in these times, complacently,/walkmans plugged to our ears,/computers, soap operas lulling our passions to sleep." She then lists specific issues that have moved her and her ancestors to create change. In the end, she dares her readers "to love, to dream" enough to continue their quests. My students seemed to connect to the poem — to the richness of its language, the urgency of its message, and its rap-like flow.

After reading the poem in class, students brainstormed for their own "Who Is Singing This Song" poem by drawing a line down the middle of a sheet of paper. On one side, they named the issues important to their lives. On the other, they listed personal experiences that shaped these concerns. As this is difficult for some students, I supplied examples — racial profiling, the environment, fair treatment of people with disabilities — and told them to talk through why a person might care about each, and then write their own. On the back of the sheet, students listed the books, songs, movies, and role models that represented their beliefs. On the bottom, students filled in the sentence "I am...." Responses ranged from "a student athlete" to "a dark poet," from "rebellious" to "macaroni and cheese." In the following days, students learned literary terms and then began the process of pre-writing, then writing a rough draft, soliciting a peer edit, and

language political?" Over the years, I have varied the first text I use depending on the students in the classroom. I know I want to get to Ebonics, or Spoken Soul, but I discovered along the way that *Pygmalion* is a better way to start — far away from Portland, Oregon.

Either way I begin, I outline the key reading and writing tasks I want students to complete during the unit; I am concerned with the content I am teaching as well as the literacy skills the students are developing. Typically, a unit in my class will take five or six weeks, and I want to make sure that students are writing a personal narrative, some poetry, and an essay during that unit.

— Linda Christensen

reworking it into a final poem. On the last day of the unit, students participated in a "read-around" as described in *Reading, Writing, and Rising Up*, listening to each poem and writing positive comments, then passing the comments to each author at the end of class.

I learned many facts about the students through this unit. I learned that I had to deal with the derogatory behavior and assumptions students had created about themselves through the reinforcement of prior classroom experiences. I learned that students could arrive in and disappear from my classes without warning. I learned that many students had not retained "the basics" — sentence structure, how to write a standardized-test-ready essay, literary terms — that they would need to move ahead in their academic educations.

So, backed by a selection of tenth-grade books that often felt like choosing the better of many evils, I set out to combine what already existed with resources from the library, my own books, and the collections of other English department teachers. For example, after focusing on the role of conflict in *The Lord of the Flies*, students watched Anna Deveare Smith's video *Twilight: Los Angeles*, based on interviews Smith conducted after the 1992 Rodney King beating. After conducting their own interviews about Rodney King with family members and school personnel and watching the video, my students wrote narratives from their own perspectives about conflicts in their lives. Then students chose the point of view of another agent of conflict in the narrative — a person, nature, fate, society — and inserted that agent's view. Throughout, I sought to help students use writing and literature to feel compassion for people involved in conflicts in the larger world and in their lives.

Making Connections

Next I wanted students to see a connection between literature, writing, and others in their community. Built on a unit designed by Esmé Schwall and Tara Affolter, teachers who were also new to East High School's English department that year, my English 10 students read Sandra Cisneros' *The House on Mango Street* in thematic parts, then responded by writing a personal vignette that shared each theme. At the end, students edited and designed their own books, each with cover, illustrations, and author biography. I delivered the books to Lori Nelson, whose eighth graders had also read *The House on Mango Street*. The middle school kids packed the high schoolers' books with letters and poems responding to what they had written. I remember the silence as the tenth graders read the responses that thanked them for sharing their stories, being brave, and being role models. Martellious, whose book featured stories of losing friends and family to violence in Chicago, told me it was one of the proudest days of his life. I knew he understood how writing about the struggles in his life could help him connect with others. While I couldn't verbalize it at the time, I now realize that giving the students opportunities to read and write for a larger audience validated them as literate, compassionate members of society.

Throughout the year, I created opportunities for students to experience literacy outside of the classroom. I wanted to take away the mystique of college, and to show them that their lives fit into an academic world. Mid-year, I coordinated with graduate student Nikola Hobbel to take a group of my ninth graders to the University of Wisconsin–Madison to be part of her teacher education young adult literature class's discussion on controversies about teaching Harper Lee's *To Kill a Mockingbird*. Bolstered by this experience, I took a carload of Period 3 students to hear Angie Cardamone, a preservice teacher who spent time each week working in my classroom, give a presentation at the university about the effects of tracking in East's English 10 classes. As Michael, Janet, and Charlie listened to Angie, they recognized their voices in her recommendations. I remember Michael, a lower-income, African-American student sitting on the side of the room, surrounded by young, white, female preservice teachers. When he participated in a discussion about how white teachers could increase "minority student achievement," I knew his confidence to speak in an academic community showed that he saw himself as a literate member of the discussion.

> ## VOICES
> ### FROM THE CLASSROOM
>
> "START SMALL. IF THERE is one teacher with whom you experience pedagogical rapport, consider yourself lucky. Do collaborative projects with each other. Eventually two of you working together will lead to three will lead to four. You will then begin to have a critical mass from which to try out new things."
>
> — Dale Weiss

How can I get started using poems with my students?

Poetry fits into every nook and cranny of the school day and school year. Sometimes a poem helps students learn about each other. A poem like George Ella Lyon's "Where I'm From" acts as a model for students to write similar poems using the details of their lives. Lyon's poem uses a repeating line and a list, which is a powerful but easy way to help students write their own poetry. (See *Reading, Writing, and Rising Up.*)

And sometimes a poem creates a word and emotional picture so that students can understand a contemporary or historical situation. The poem "teaches" an event from a different perspective. For example, Martín Espada's poem "Federico's Ghost," included in *Rethinking Globalization,* illuminates the effects of pesticide sprays on farmworkers and their children.

Students also can use poetry to demonstrate their understanding of a historical or literary character or situation: I often recycle Lyon's "Where I'm From" poem and have students write from a particular character's point of view.

Dialogue poems (see *Rethinking Our Classrooms, Volume 1*) are effective when controversy or different opinions may arise. For example, students may write about the integration of Central High School in Little Rock, Arkansas, from the point of view of either a segregationist or an integrationist on the first day of school. These help students get inside the heads and hearts of people from literature and history.

But poetry shouldn't be limited to the reading and writing of poems. Poetry is also the play of language in essays and narratives. It encompasses hearing the heartbeat of a sentence, finding and using strong verbs, sliding metaphoric language into an analytic essay, surprising the reader with an unexpected analogy.

— Linda Christensen

The books mentioned here are published by Rethinking Schools. Details can be found beginning on page 66.

Near the end of the year, I wanted students to find connections between their lives and a seemingly unrelated text. So to preface the reading of Chinua Achebe's novel *Things Fall Apart,* students studied Nigerian folktales and performed them for our class. Then I asked an African storytelling professor from UW–Madison to speak to the students. Angie Cardamone agreed to pick the professor up on campus; a student volunteered to videotape the presentation; I organized volunteers to set up the room. When I got sick, I arranged for a sub I knew to cover the class, and trusted that my students could hold the event together.

Sure enough, the students raved and the professor praised the attention and maturity they showed. And though they complained about the difficulty of the reading, the tediousness of text coding (a reading strategy described in Cris Tovani's excellent book *I Read It, but I Don't Get It: Comprehension Strategies for Adolescent Readers*), and the very idea of a "literary analysis" essay, my Period 3 students held on. As I look back on this unit, I realize that the students had gained enough confidence in themselves to tackle — and maybe even enjoy — a difficult read.

Sure, only a few students would routinely do work outside of class, and a lack of computer access caused many projects to be late. Sure, I had to wait for the kids to stop talking at the beginning of every class. Sometimes yelling helped, sometimes walking out, shutting the door behind me, and then walking back in with exaggerated gestures of "Good morning!" did the trick. Things were rarely easy, but by the end of the school year, I witnessed something remarkable that made it all worth the pain.

Conclusions

On the last day of class, I asked the students to read the poems they had written about each other. One by one, the students read loudly and slowly. When Brittany, a quiet, white, middle-class girl who loved the ballet, finished reading her poem about Janet, an extroverted African-American girl from a low-income family who loved Tupac Shakur, Janet gave her a hug. The students began a pattern of reading and walking the poems over to the classmates they'd written about, often wrapping their arms around each other. And when their poems were read, I was surprised to see my toughest boys cry.

After the reading, I started to stand but was shushed down by

Michael. "Wait, Ms. Wagner," he said, rising, "I've got something to say." Student by student, Michael trailed his finger around the circle, saying one good thing about every one in it. Sometimes I didn't get the jokes, but it was clear that the students understood. He finished, and another student picked up the routine, often walking to the student in the spotlight, hugging, smiling, or hitting a shoulder with a fist. I remember what the students said to each other, and what they said to me.

In the last minutes of Period 3, I sat back and watched the class function as a community of caring individuals. I marveled that I didn't have to say a word. ■

All students' names have been changed, unless permission was given.

References

The House on Mango Street, by Sandra Cisneros (New York: Vintage Contemporaries, 1984).

I Read It, but I Don't Get It: Comprehension Strategies for Adolescent Readers, by Cris Tovani (Portland, ME: Stenhouse Publishers, 2000).

Reading, Writing, and Rising Up: Teaching About Social Justice and the Power of the Written Word, by Linda Christensen (Milwaukee: Rethinking Schools, 2000). See page 68 for details.

Things Fall Apart, by Chinua Achebe (New York: Anchor Books, 1994).

Twilight: Los Angeles, by Anna Deveare Smith (New York: Offline Video and PBS Entertainment, 2000).

"Who Is Singing This Song?" by Janice Mirikitani as published in *Yell-Oh Girls! Emerging Voices Explore Culture, Identity, and Growing Up Asian American,* edited by Vickie Nam (New York: HarperCollins, 2001).

Making Rules

I admit it, I was naïve. Before I started teaching first grade I believed I wouldn't have to make any specific rules for my class. I believed that if I simply treated my students with respect they would naturally respond respectfully, and that would take care of things.

It didn't take long for me to realize I was wrong. In fact I realized it on my very first day.

My first act as a teacher was to corral my students into some semblance of a straight line on the playground and lead them to our classroom, where a big and colorful "Welcome to Room 13" sign adorned the door. One of the kids, Fred, took one look at the sign and said: "Thirteen is an unlucky number. I don't want to be here." I managed a half-smile and ushered the kids, reluctant Fred included, into the room.

I then directed the students to sit in a circle on the brightly colored rug that lay in front of the semi-circle of tiny desks. I had bought this rug a few days before at Goodwill, thrilled as I'd imagined it as the home to hours and hours of wonderful conversations and learning.

Lizzi and Angela started dancing in circles. "No, please *sit* in a circle," I said, to which Angela responded: "When we stop twirling in our circles we fall down. Then we sit up in the place that we fell down." A few other students sat down at desks.

BY
DALE
WEISS

A small group of boys started playing with puzzles. Another group of boys and girls began trying on clothes in the housekeeping area. Six other students were sitting in a corner of the room playing hand-clapping games. Granted, they were sitting in a circle, but not on the rug.

Unbelievable, I thought. How could a direction as straightforward as "please sit in a circle on the rug" be so completely misunderstood, playfully re-invented, or simply ignored?

I was at a loss. And things didn't get better that day. My room was chaos surrounded by four walls and a door.

By the end of the day I was a "born again rule maker." I felt that while my aspiration to have a rule-free classroom had been a good one, it was nonetheless based more on idealism than on what these 6- and 7-year-old children could handle. I didn't want to be the kind of teacher for whom "well-behaved" equals "silent and still." Yet I also wanted my classroom to be less chaotic, though not by totally squelching all the energy and enthusiasm the kids were bringing through my door.

I wanted to create a structure that fostered a safe and well-run classroom community, one that taught students the levels of responsibility that were necessary to experience various levels of freedom, and one in which the voices of students were included as part of the process.

Yes, I would need to make rules after all.

Learning from Chaos

After that first day — much of which I'd spent glaring at nametag after nametag in an effort to separate out those causing trouble from the innocent bystanders — I learned my students' names faster than I

VOICES FROM THE CLASSROOM

"I'M A YOUNG MAN BUT sometimes in school I feel like I'm a grandma in a hurricane. At the end of the day I walk home and sit down on my couch and I think, 'What the hell was that?' You always have to be on. You never quite know what that kindergartner is going to say or ask you, or what that eighth grader is going to blurt out in the classroom. You've got to be ready for it."

— Steve Vande Zande

have ever memorized anything in my life. On the second day I greeted each student at the door by name.

Then I told each of them to please sit down at his or her desk. I made it clear I was telling them to do it, not asking. I was polite but firm. Perhaps because of this, and because the direction I gave them was more concrete — "there is your chair, please sit on it," as opposed to asking them to work with 20-plus other kids to create a circle — the students quickly complied.

After taking attendance and the lunch count, I told the students that we were going to talk about how our first day of school had gone. Brett started talking about his first day of kindergarten. Aha, I thought. Once again I had forgotten that students, especially young children, need directions to be very, very explicit. So I rephrased my question: "Yesterday was our first day of first grade together. Please tell me some things you liked about the day."

"The toasted cheese at lunch was pretty good," said Fred. "I learned to do double-dutch on the playground," responded Lisa. "I'm glad that Lizzi and I are in the same class again," piped in Lindsey. Ah, food and friendship: the cornerstones of first grade.

Then I asked if they could think of anything that they did not like about their first day of first grade. Hesitation. Finally Angela broke the silence. "It was kind of crazy in here. Like everybody was running around too much." John added: "We could never do that in kindergarten, and if we did, we had to fold our hands together and not even say one word." Lisa chimed in: "And if we did say a word, we had a big time-out in the corner of the room."

Jacob, who the day before had spoken so softly that his words were barely audible, began to cry. "What's wrong, Jacob?" I asked. He started sobbing. His words did not come. I asked if anyone knew why Jacob was crying. John responded: "He used to get in trouble all the time in kindergarten."

I asked the students to tell me if they felt safe in our classroom yesterday. A variety of responses followed:

"Not exactly, because the kids were getting into lots of fights."

"I felt tired because it was too loud in here."

"I was safe because I carried my scissors the right way."

"In kindergarten our teacher told us what to do all the time. You didn't tell us those things so I didn't know if it was OK to do some stuff."

"I liked the housekeeping area but I think there were too many kids in there because we kept fighting about who got to cook the eggs."

"I did some stuff that I did in kindergarten, like throw some Lego blocks. But in kindergarten I got time-outs but yesterday I didn't."

The comments went on and on. I gained many insights. For one, my students had been heavily exposed to rules and consequences during kindergarten. And secondly, the students seemed to be asking for structure.

Drawing Up Rules

I then told my students to once again sit on the rug in a circle. But this time, before anyone left their desks, I explained what a circle was and how they would form one, step by step. Then, as gently as possible, I helped my students place their bodies in a roughly circle-like

How do I get a student to redo an assignment?

Redoing or revising an assignment is key for students who lack academic skills. When we allow students to slide by with shoddy, inferior work, C or D papers, we set them up for future failure.

Establishing clear criteria for each assignment — and going over those criteria with students before they get started on their work — helps with the revision process. Students need to know specifically what the teacher's expectations are. No guessing. Students need both clarity and models when possible.

Prior to assigning a poem, literary analysis, or response to a film or book, I hand out criteria sheets, which list the traits of the genre, and examples of student work from previous years. If I don't have examples, I write a sample model to distribute. If the criteria are clear, then students can use them as a guide when they revise. For example, I have my students color-highlight their papers for different narrative criteria; when they have no dialogue or character description to highlight, they know that is a place where they need to revise. The revision is part of the process of writing, and I build it into each assignment.

configuration on the rug. And I sat down in the circle myself and modeled appropriate behaviors for circle time: One person talks at a time; listen with your ears and your whole body when someone else is speaking; don't fidget; be respectful of other people's space, and so on.

Once we were finally in a circle I said: "Who can tell me what you think is needed to make our classroom a safe place to be?" Lots of hands went up.

"We don't hit each other."

"We share."

"Everybody gets invited to the birthday parties."

"At recess we don't trip other kids or laugh if they fall down."

I redirected the conversation a bit, reminding students that for now I only wanted to talk about what we needed to do to make our classroom a safe place. The comments continued.

"We listen if somebody is saying something."

"We don't make fun of other kids."

"If somebody wants to use my crayons I would let them."

"We are respectful."

I wrote all of their responses on a big sheet of butcher paper. The list was long and contained many great ideas. I hung it on the wall and told the kids to look at all their answers and think of one idea that was more important than all the others. They chose: "We are respectful."

(See "Childhood Narratives" and "Essay with an Attitude" in *Reading, Writing, and Rising Up*. For more information on this book see page 68.)

Sometimes, especially in an untracked classroom, some students will complete the assignment thoroughly, while others will attempt the assignment but get bogged down or run into roadblocks. It's easy to blame students at this point: to say they are lazy, or "slow," or lack a serious interest in school. Instead of bemoaning what they've done incorrectly, we can use their papers to figure out where their comprehension broke down. This is when the real teaching begins. Students are more likely to return to a task when they understand it.

— Linda Christensen

After carefully directing the kids back into their seats, I placed three items on each of their desks: sheets of lined paper with space at the top for drawings, a pencil, and a set of large crayons (the kind that is easier for young children to use). I told the students to use the unlined space on their paper to draw a picture of something they would be doing if they were being respectful. Before asking the students to begin drawing, we brainstormed a list of possible examples. I told them that they had great ideas and that their drawings didn't need to look the same — in fact they shouldn't.

Students then brought their pictures back up to our rug space. They were still somewhat clumsy about forming a circle but they managed it this time without step-by-step instruction. They each shared their drawings, explaining what they would do to show they were being respectful. Amanda drew a picture of herself helping another student tie her shoe. Lindsey drew a group of children sitting in a circle reading together. Brett's drawing showed several students taking turns cooking the make-believe eggs in the housekeeping area.

Back at their seats, I wrote under each drawing the words that the student wanted to accompany the picture. While I was going around the room doing this, each student drew borders along the periphery of their page. This kept them occupied while I worked one-on-one with each student.

Then we arranged the pages in quilt form on our classroom wall. We referred to this as our "Acting Appropriately Wall." (I frequently used the word "appropriate" with my students, and made sure they understood its meaning as well as the actions that brought the meaning to life.) The next day Fred said: "I think that wall is like our classroom rules. We only have one rule but the rule has lots of parts to it." Fred was right. From his first-grade vantage point, being respectful of others was central to everything else we were doing.

What if Someone Breaks the Rules?

Later that week we began to talk about what should be done if someone in the class chose not to follow our classroom rule of respect. By now I had learned that things needed to be carefully laid out in a clear, concise, step-by-step manner. Again, I told the students to come up to the rug and sit in a circle. (I had purchased tiny carpet squares to use for circle time. Each child took a carpet square and placed it on the rug to mark their sitting spot. This helped to more clearly define the space each student would occupy.) I began by asking what should be done if someone in our class didn't act in a respectful way. To help make the conversation less threatening, I used myself as an example first. "Let's say I choose to not write in my journal during journal time and instead I choose to start playing with the puzzles. What do you think my consequence should be?" Lots of hands went up.

"I think you shouldn't get to play with the puzzles for the rest of the year."

"You should have to write in your journal during recess time."

"You would have to be last in line to recess."

"No recess for a week."

"You could get a warning but if you do it again, you'll get a bigger punishment."

I believe that consequences should be logical and address the misbehavior that has occurred. I also believe that consequences should help to redirect behavior so that students can begin to internalize appropriate behaviors. I do not believe that external consequences — in and of themselves — do much good in any kind of long-lasting way.

I told my students that they'd come up with a great list of consequences, and now I wanted us to decide on one consequence for the inappropriate choice I'd made during journal time. I explained that the consequence needed to help me figure out what I had done wrong and what a more appropriate choice would have been. And if some kind of punishment was appropriate, it needed to make sense for what I had done wrong. Because I was the teacher, I would ultimately decide what the punishment would be (even for myself!). But I made it clear to students that I wanted and valued their input.

After much discussion, the students decided that two things needed to happen. First, I should be reminded that during journal time I was supposed to be writing in my journal, not playing with other toys in the classroom. And second, because I was playing during part of journal time, I should write in my journal during part of free-choice time. I was very pleased. The consequence addressed my misbehavior and was logical.

The students then took turns participating in a role-play depicting my misbehavior and the consequence I was given. Afterwards, a few students drew a picture of the misbehavior and the appropriate consequence we had decided upon. This picture became the first entry in our "Consequence Wall," which was displayed adjacent to our "Acting Appropriately Wall." This same process was followed when addressing other misbehaviors and consequences.

Now admittedly this was a pretty straightforward example. My "misbehavior" was not all that serious, and there was a way to deal with it within our classroom and within the confines of the same school day.

I realized I would also need to address misbehaviors of a more serious nature with my students. For example, what if one student physically harmed another student? Many of these kinds of infractions were clearly addressed in a handbook on expected student behaviors that was provided by my school. I decided to broaden our discussion on classroom rules to include the concept of schoolwide rules and consequences.

What was important to me at this point was that my students were getting exposed to the basic ideas of rules and consequences, and they were getting a chance to practice applying those ideas. It was a first step.

Even with the classroom rules and consequences firmly in place, things did not always run smoothly. My students needed to be reminded constantly what appropriate behaviors looked like and sounded like. We had daily discussions regarding this. During that first year of my career I learned about the incredible amount of time and consistency that is needed to help students learn to internalize appropriate behaviors. Eventually, students became less and less dependent on me for guidance in terms of their behavior, as they learned to rely more both on themselves and each other. Though the ride was bumpy many times, the outcome was well worth it. ∎

The Desecration
of Studs Terkel

FIGHTING CENSORSHIP AND
SELF-CENSORSHIP

It began with a call that I was to report to the vice-principal's office as soon as possible. The voice at the other end indicated that it was urgent.

I was a first-year teacher at Grant High School in Portland, Oregon. The call gave me the creeps. From the moment we met I'd felt that Lloyd Dixon, the curriculum VP, could look deep into my soul — and that he didn't like what he saw. Whenever we passed in the hall he smiled at me thinly, but with a glance that said: "I've got your number, Bigelow." He had a drawl that reminded me of the Oklahoma highway patrolman who gleefully arrested me in 1971 for not carrying my draft card.

It was my first year as a teacher. And I must confess, my classroom difficulties made me a tad paranoid.

Dixon's secretary ushered me into his office when I arrived. "It seems we have a problem, Bill," he said. He paused to look at me and make sure I was duly appreciative of the serious nature of the meeting. "The mother of a student of yours, Dorothy Jennings, called to say that you had given her smutty material, a book that discusses oral sex. What's the story?"

I explained to the vice-principal that the "smutty" material was Studs Terkel's *Working*, a

BY
BILL
BIGELOW

book that includes interviews with dozens of people — auto workers, hotel clerks, washroom attendants, musicians — who describe what they do for a living and how they feel about it. I told him that it was a text the school had purchased and that I issued it to my ninth graders for some in-class reading during our career education study.

"Well, Bill, Dorothy apparently took the book home. And her mother's upset because of a section Dorothy read her about a prostitute, where she describes having oral sex."

I told him that I had not assigned that chapter and that students didn't have permission to take the books home, as I taught two sections of the class but had only 35 copies of the book. I didn't mention that indeed I had considered using the chapter, "Roberta Victor, Hooker," because it was filled with insights about sexism, law, and hypocrisy. (The alleged oral sex description was a brief reference in a long interview.)

Dixon ordered me to bring him a copy of *Working* so that he could read the passages I assigned, and to meet with him the next day. "You should be aware that I regard this as a serious situation," he said. And with that, New Teacher was waved out the door.

I went to see my friend Tom McKenna, a member of a support group I'd helped organize among teachers in the area. Tom suggested I talk to our union rep. My visit with Thurston Ohman, a big-hearted man with an easy from-the-belly laugh, was a revelation. "You haven't done anything wrong," he assured me. "If they try to come after you in some way, the union will back you 100%."

Solidarity

It was a delicious moment, and I realized how utterly alone I'd felt up until that point. Ironically, in my history classes and my freshman social studies classes we'd recently studied the rise of labor unions, but until that instant I'd never personally been a beneficiary of the "injury to one is an injury to all" solidarity.

Buoyed by my talk with Ohman, I returned to VP Dixon's office the next day. He wasn't worried about Mrs. Jennings anymore. But he was still upset. "Bill, I read over the pieces that you assigned. Very interesting. Pretty negative stuff. My daughter is an airline stewardess. She doesn't feel like the gal in that book.

"Do you know that the reading on the auto worker uses the s-word five times and the f-word once?"

"The s-word?"I asked.

"Yes. On pages 258, 259, 261 and twice on page 262. The f-word is used on page 265."

I didn't want to laugh, but I didn't know what to say. His complaint was about an interview with Gary Bryner, president of the United Auto Workers local at the Lordstown, Ohio, General Motors plant. Given Mr. Dixon's comment about his daughter, I had a hunch that his ire was aimed more at Bryner's "negative" critique of the plant's deadening working conditions and his descriptions of workers' resistance than at his occasional use of s- and f-words. But this wasn't the time or place to argue politics. "I guess I didn't realize, Mr. Dixon."

"No. Well, Bill, here's what I'd like you to do. Get a black marker and every time this gentleman uses the s- and f-words, darken them so students won't be exposed to that kind of language. Will you do that for me, Bill?"

I know some people would have fought it. Had it not been my first year as a teacher — a temporary teacher, no less — I would have fought. Instead I made one of those compromises that we're not proud of, but that we make so we can live to fight another day. After school, marker in hand, I cleansed Gary Bryner of his foul language — in all 35 copies of *Working*.

Twenty-some years later, the censored books are still in circulation in Portland high schools.

I offer this instance of curricular interference as a way of acknowledging that administrative repression can be a factor limiting the inventiveness of a new teacher. But in my experience, the intrusions of the Lloyd Dixons of the world are exceptions that prove the rule. And the rule is that we have an enormous amount of freedom.

Even as a first-year teacher the Jennings affair was my only brush with administrative censure. I frequently brought in controversial guest speakers, films, and additional readings. It was 1978-79, the year of Three Mile Island, the final months of the Sandinista revolution in Nicaragua, and a growing U.S. awareness of the injustices of South African apartheid. In class, we studied all of these.

No doubt, it's important for individuals early in their teaching careers, as well as those of us further along, to make an assessment of the political context in which we work. After all, if we lose our job, we don't do anyone any good. But generally, I believe that the most powerful agent of censorship lives in our own heads, and we almost always have more freedom than we use. The great Brazilian educator Paulo Freire once wrote that in schools we should attempt to fill up all the political space we're given. But we rarely do.

That said, a few years ago a school district in an affluent Portland suburb terminated a good friend of mine at the completion of her third year of probation, spouting nonsense about her failure to teach critical thinking skills and the like. The obvious irony for those of us at her hearing was that she was fired precisely because she was successful at teaching her students to think critically. She had the misfortune of being one of the only non-tenured teachers in a progressive, pedagogically adventurous social studies department during the rise of the ferociously conservative Oregon Citizens Alliance. The political environment had shifted to the right; it was sacrificial lamb time.

It's worth mentioning that during my first years at Jefferson High School, following my year at Grant, I was gifted with supervising vice-principals who were extraordinarily supportive and even enthusiastic about livelier, risk-taking teaching. Shirley Glick was one of several VPs who offered nothing but encouragement as I felt my way toward a more critical and multicultural curriculum. The Lloyd Dixons of the world exist, but so do the Shirley Glicks.

Incidentally, I never met Mrs. Jennings. But she left her mark. For a long time I subconsciously imagined a Mrs. Jennings sitting at every student's home, hoping for a chance to chew me out for some teaching crime I'd committed: "You snake, why'd you use that book/film/article/poem with my innocent child?"

In my imagination, parents were potential opponents, not allies, and I avoided calling them to talk about their children or what I was trying to teach. This neglect was a bad habit to fall into. Even from a narrow classroom management standpoint, my failure to call moms, dads, or grandparents from time to time made my quest for classroom order a lonely campaign. Parents could have exerted a bit of pressure on the home front. But they also could have told me something about their son or daughter, offered a fuller portrait than what I saw in my daily slice of 47 minutes.

And that would likely have made me a more effective teacher. ∎

How to Teach Controversial Content And Not Get Fired

A classmate in my master's degree program explained to our class: "I really want to talk with my students about why it's wrong to discriminate against gay people. I had one conversation with them about it, but then my principal found out, and ever since then he's been watching every move I make. I feel like I can't teach about this any more."

After working for weeks to write units on such topics as gender bias, racism, and the criminalization of youth, our class discussed what it would be like to actually teach these units in our classroom. We wanted to teach the lessons we'd written — in fact, we had chosen this master's program because it explicitly focused on anti-racist teaching. But while many of my classmates strongly believed in the lessons we wrote, at the same time most expressed doubts about actually being able to teach these lessons in our classrooms.

Our professor prompted us: "Tell me about your fears. What do you think could happen if you were to teach these units in your classrooms?" We called out our concerns and our professor wrote our list on the board:

BY
KELLEY
DAWSON
SALAS

- I'll get fired.
- My principal won't fire me but will retaliate against me in other ways.

- Other teachers in the building won't want to work with me.
- I'll end up being totally isolated at my school.
- Parents will challenge me.

These fears are very real for teachers who decide that curriculum needs to integrate a strong social justice focus, one that helps kids learn about multiple perspectives and develop critical thinking skills.

Even after completing my fifth year of teaching, I still experience fears and insecurities when it comes to implementing a social justice curriculum. But it's gotten a little easier each year.

Out on a Limb

During my first year of teaching, I was inspired by an article in the journal *Rethinking Schools* by Kate Lyman about teaching the Civil Rights Movement to elementary students. (To read the article visit www.rethinkingschools.org/newteacher.) Using Kate's article as a starting point, I decided to teach a unit on the Civil Rights Movement and have my third-grade students write and prepare a class play for presentation at our February all-school assembly, which had a "black history" theme.

I knew that I was going out on a limb, because I wrote the unit myself, and I really didn't know whether I was "allowed" to deviate from the third-grade social studies textbook I was supposed to be using. As I began teaching the unit I felt isolated: I had asked my partner teacher to plan the unit with me and to teach it simultaneously in his classroom, but he'd decided he wasn't interested in doing that.

Despite my feelings of uneasiness, I went ahead with my teaching and found that the students responded very well to the content and the projects that we did. But I still wondered what consequences I might face if someone walked into my classroom and began to question what we were studying.

The story had a happy ending. My partner teacher — although he politely declined my request to co-teach the unit — saw that I needed some help, and so after school one afternoon we built a life-sized "bus" for the play. The kids wrote the play, learned their parts, and in the process showed a good understanding of the events of the Montgomery, Alabama, bus boycott.

The students presented their play at our February assembly, and as a final touch after the performance, they sang Bob Marley's "Get Up, Stand Up" and got the whole school up and singing along. A strange feeling washed over me. I had embarked on this unit with a sense of fear and insecurity, yet with a kind of determination that what I was doing made sense. Things turned out much better than I had expected. It was a far cry from "What if I get fired for this?" This was a good lesson for me. I was at a school that was not particularly progressive, yet I learned that it wasn't repressive, either. It was mostly a "teach and let teach" environment. I never took any flak for teaching about the Civil Rights Movement, though neither did I get any earth-shattering compliments. Teachers didn't start knocking down my door asking to team-teach social studies units with me, but neither did my principal ask me to go back to the textbook. In short, what I had done was OK.

> **VOICES FROM THE CLASSROOM**
>
> "IT'S IN THE CLASSROOM where we mainly do our activism, instilling in the kids a sense of justice and acceptance of different cultures and races. Whenever someone says a put-down about someone else, and we sit down and talk about it, that's activism to me."
>
> — Floralba Vivas

Seeking "Permission"

Since then, I have talked to lots of veteran teachers and asked how I should go about teaching from a social justice perspective, given that I am a new teacher with many things to learn. I want to teach my students to think critically, analyze our world, and learn to change it, but I am not always as confident about my approach as I wish I was. And I often second-guess myself, wondering whether I am "allowed" to teach the way I want to teach. At the end of my first year of teaching, I asked veteran social studies teacher Bill Bigelow a question that had been on my mind all year: "Who has the authority to decide what I teach?"

He answered simply: "You do."

It was a critical moment for me. All year I had been searching for someone who would grant me permission to teach the way I wanted to. In my school community, I had not experienced resistance, but I was looking for more than the absence of resistance. I needed someone to tell me that it was OK to do the kind of social justice teaching I was trying to work toward. My conversation with Bill made me understand that the person who has the greatest control over what happens in my classroom is me. Waiting for someone else to give me permission or authority to teach the way I wanted to was not necessary.

But that's not to say that those of us who wish to teach from a social justice perspective don't need to explain our curriculum and methods to others in our school community. We need to be prepared to respond to questioning or criticism from other teachers, administrators, or parents who don't want us to teach in this way. Peter Brown, a teacher-educator from California, gave me some great advice that he said he shares regularly with those he mentors: "Before you start a unit that you think may be controversial, inform the parents and principal about what you'll be teaching and explain how it fits into the school's curriculum and standards."

For example, the Milwaukee Public Schools' Teaching and Learning Goal #1 states: "Students will project anti-racist, anti-biased attitudes through their participation in a multilingual, multi-ethnic, culturally diverse curriculum." This provides an excellent rationale for many of the activities I do in my classroom, and since my district is formally committed to it, it's hard for principals and parents to argue.

At times I have used an approach of notifying parents and my principal ahead of time. Other times, when I was fairly certain there wouldn't be resistance to my teaching, I have followed a philosophy of "teach first, answer questions later." For example, I used this approach with a video called "That's a Family." The video is an excellent resource for teaching about family diversity. It presents several types of families, including adoptive families, single parent families, foster families, gay and lesbian families, and divorced families. (For more information see www.rethinkingschools.org/newteacher.)

VOICES FROM THE CLASSROOM

"WE HAVE TO TEACH from a global perspective. We work in the biggest superpower on the planet. Given increased global inequality, global warming, and poverty, and the devastation of mother earth, we have responsibilities to address that. We need to teach for global justice. And if we don't, who will?"

— Bob Peterson

Before I began using this video with my class, I cleared it with my principal (I needed her permission to purchase the video for our school library). I also considered whether I should notify parents that I would be teaching about different kinds of families, including gay and lesbian families. I predicted there could be some resistance from parents who are opposed to homosexuality. I asked one parent what she thought I should do. "Do you notify parents of every single thing you teach?" she asked. " If not, it would be inconsistent to notify them about this, and could raise more alarm than necessary." I agreed with her analysis and have taught the video two years in a row without complaint from anyone.

Other Suggestions

Part of the process of deciding whether to use a video (or any other material or lesson) also involves having an understanding of the school community where you work. After my first year, I switched schools and I now work at a very progressive school with teachers and families who are, for the most part, committed to diversity and social justice. At this school, people are much more likely to be tolerant.

As with any kind of curriculum you teach, a unit you write yourself should be of high quality and well-prepared. In planning units that address specific issues of social justice, I have found it useful to start by researching what other teachers have done in this same area. There is *lots* of social justice curriculum out there. Rethinking Schools and Teaching for Change are two great resources, where I have regularly found and "borrowed" from other teachers' teaching ideas. (For links see www.rethinkingschools.org/newteacher.)

Another very important rule of thumb is to always preview any materials that you are going to use, even if they have been recommended by other teachers. I found that when I taught my unit on the Civil Rights Movement, much of the PBS *Eyes on the Prize* video series was useful and appropriate for my third graders. Other parts were not as crucial and some, such as graphic images of the corpse of lynching victim Emmett Till, were not age-appropriate.

In my first few years as a teacher, I have taught about several different issues that some people might consider controversial. They include immigrants' experiences and rights, union organizing, the Civil Rights Movement, Mexican-American organizing, resistance to slavery, the U.S. government's removal of Native Americans from their ancestral lands, the U.S. war on Iraq, the budget shortage in our schools, bullying, stereotypes, xenophobia, homophobia, racism, and sexism.

By no means have I done a full "unit" on each of these topics. Some, such as slavery and the removal of Native Americans from their lands, I teach through literature. Others, like stereotypes and racism, require a long-term conversation with my students. And some, like our study of the U.S. war on Iraq and the budget shortage in our schools, come up during our regular classroom discussions of current events.

Each year I try to improve and add on to the units or concepts that I've taught in the previous year, but I still feel I have a long way to go to reach my goal of having a year's worth of solid curriculum that integrates a social justice perspective and teaches about specific issues of justice. Knowing that I am making progress and that I have the support of like-minded teachers keeps me energized to continue working toward my goals.

Engaging my students in social justice issues is, for me, at the heart of my teaching. I have learned that developing curriculum is a long-term process that often happens very slowly. But I wouldn't do it any other way. ■

The Power of Songs
In the Classroom

Songs, like poetry, can be powerful teaching tools. The lyrical metaphors, rhythms, and stories in many songs motivate and educate students. It's amazing what students will remember from a song, as compared to what they forget from a teacher talking.

Like poetry, songs can be used in many classroom activities. They can spur further study and research or be incorporated into class performances. They are also a great way to smooth a transition from one activity to another or to begin a class period.

I introduce a new "song of the week" each Monday and give students a copy of the lyrics to keep in the three-ring binder they use to collect much of my alternative curriculum. (For more details on the binder idea see "Getting Your Classroom Together," page 26.) We start each morning with the song, and usually within a day or two the children are singing along — regardless of the musical genre. Despite my questionable singing capability, I sing along too. Teachers who are more self-conscious or who don't wish to sing can identify a couple of students with good voices and encourage them to lead the class.

BY
BOB
PETERSON

Sometimes I use a song to introduce a unit of study; other times I use a song to emphasize a particular point in a lesson.

When I introduce a song, I go over the geo-

133

graphical connections using a classroom wall map. I also discuss any vocabulary that might be difficult. Finally, and most importantly, I make sure the context of the song is set. Depending on whether I use the song at the beginning of a unit of study or in the middle, the amount of "context setting" varies greatly. For example, I use Nancy Schimmel's "1492" which includes the line "But someone was already here" as a way to encourage students to think more critically about the Columbus myth. Similarly I use Tracy Chapman's "Why" as a way to introduce a problem-posing approach to curriculum, as Chapman asks such provocative questions as: "Why do the babies starve when there's enough food to feed the world?" and "Why when there's so many of us are there people still alone?"

The lyrics of virtually any song can be found on the web with a bit of Googling. Finding a free (and legal) MP3 download of the actual song is a bit harder — but worth the effort. Don't be intimidated if you've never downloaded a song or burned a CD. Ask a friend or a teenager and you'll probably find someone who can help you.

Public libraries are another good source for finding CDs — especially if your library system has a searchable online catalog. I prefer to have a copy of the songs I use on a CD, either one that I've purchased, downloaded, or copied — all legally of course!

For several different annotated listing of songs useful in the classroom check out www.rethinkingschools.org/newteacher. ■

CHAPTER THREE

Getting to Know the Kids

Field Trip

On a hot, humid Wednesday in July, I tag along with a group of 100 second- and third-grade students on a field trip to the University of California–Los Angeles. The students attend 75th Street Elementary School, located in South Central Los Angeles. I spend a lot of time at this school, conducting research, making friends, and learning. Some teachers thought it would be a good idea for the students to see the campus, life outside the walls of South Central.

More than half of South Central's 60,000 residents live below the federal poverty line; most who attend 75th Street live at or below poverty. Unemployment is close to 20%. Single mothers raise close to one third of the children. More than a quarter of the mothers have less than a ninth-grade education.

Almost as soon as the kids bound off the bus, a group of students start peering through a fence. I follow them.

"What are we looking at, Emily?" I ask.

As if in unison, five students answer, "The grass!"

"Oh, Miss Becky, have you ever seen so much grass?" Emily asks me.

BY
REBECCA
CONSTANTINO

"Really green grass," Kevin adds.

"I ain't never seen so much grass in one spot,"

137

exclaims Angela. I pull them away, since we have other sites to see.

Though it is morning, it's sweltering. I suggest that we stop for a water break.

"No kid brought a water bottle, so we have to find a fountain," says Miss Suarez, their teacher.

As if on cue, the children start complaining about the heat and their thirst. We assure them that a drinking fountain is close.

As we walk to the "big steps," as Ariel calls them, I quietly ask several students why they didn't bring water bottles. I am hoping to turn the conversation into a discussion about how the body works and its need for water. Instead, I learn about economics.

"We don't never buy water in them bottles," one student tells me.

"I see the teachers with the bottles, but we don't get them; my momma says they cost too much," adds another.

Johnnie, a student from another class, tells me, "Oh, we buy water from the store, but we buy it in them big bottles."

"So your mom and dad don't like the water that comes from the sink?" I ask him.

"No, Miss Becky, we live in a garage, we don't got water."

He slips his hand into mine and, for some unknown reason, we both look up at the sky. On this day, it's so clear and blue without a hint of smog or clouds.

"Pretty sky," Johnnie says.

I concur, but even then, reality does not escape me: I am holding hands with a sweet, excited boy who lives in a garage. He has no running water, no electricity, and no money to buy a bottle of water.

We round a corner as we head off and pass a construction site. The area around it is surrounded by yellow "caution" tape. Several students run from the group to the tape. Kevin yells, "a dead body!" and several more students join him.

"Whenever you see that tape, you know somebody is dead." says Ariel.

The students are surprised to get to the yellow tape and find that there is no dead body, just construction.

Los Angeles County is one of the best illustrations of the massive gap that exists between rich and poor in this country. In Beverly Hills, the average home price is well over a million dollars, and the average income exceeds $160,000. It's only a 20-minute drive to South Central Los Angeles, one of the most densely populated areas in Los Angeles County. Alfredo, who is on this field trip, lives with nine other people in a one-bedroom apartment.

The community is plagued by violence. In the 12 square miles near 75th Street Elementary, there are at least six active gangs. I wonder about these children's futures.

Our government's education policies don't take into account that Johnnie lives in a garage, goes hungry most days, or hears gunshots most nights. Instead, politicians are concerned about his standardized test scores and at what age he will be reading. According to state standards, Johnnie should be able to "focus in identifying and recalling main ideas and supporting details in expository text ... and have complex comprehension strategies.... Furthermore, he should be able to distinguish between literary forms such as poetry and fairy tales."

I want Johnnie to read. I want him to find joy in books, but I know he won't do it as quickly as a child with access to an abundance of books (one of the best predictors of how well one reads), a light to do homework, and a full belly when he goes to bed. When Johnnie does not do well on standardized tests we blame him, his teacher, or the method with which he was taught. We don't blame the fact that he is hungry — or that we compare him to a child that lives only miles from him but is worlds apart.

We are so concerned about the standards we have set for Johnnie to meet that we have forgotten to set some for ourselves: All children should be safe. All children should have access to a quality education. No child should be hungry or want for health care. Every child should be able to play and roll in soft, green grass.

When the current administration leaves office, we will have new standards for Johnnie to meet. The grass will still be green and soft at UCLA. And I wonder if Johnnie will still be living in a garage. ∎

Taking Multicultural, Anti-Racist Education Seriously

AN INTERVIEW
WITH EDUCATOR ENID LEE

The following is condensed from an interview with Enid Lee, a consultant in anti-racist education and organizational change and author of *Letters to Marcia: A Teachers' Guide to Anti-Racist Education.* Lee is the former supervisor of race/ethnic relations for the North York Board of Education in metropolitan Toronto. She was born and raised in the Caribbean and has been working in the field of language, culture, and race for more than 25 years in Canada and the United States. She was interviewed by Barbara Miner.

What do you mean by a multicultural education?

The term multicultural education has a lot of different meanings. The term I use most often is anti-racist education.

Multicultural or anti-racist education is fundamentally a perspective. It's a point of view that cuts across all subject areas, and addresses the histories and experiences of people who have been left out of the curriculum. Its purpose is to help us deal equitably with all the cultural and racial differences that you find in the human family. It's also a perspective that allows us to get at explanations for why things are the way they are in terms of power relationships, in terms of equality issues.

So when I say multicultural or anti-racist education, I am talking

about equipping students, parents, and teachers with the tools needed to combat racism and ethnic discrimination, and to find ways to
build a society that includes all people on an equal footing.

It also has to do with how the school is run in terms of who gets
to be involved with decisions. It has to do with parents and how their
voices are heard or not heard. It has to do with who gets hired in the
school.

If you don't take multicultural education or anti-racist education
seriously, you are actually promoting a monocultural or racist education. There is no neutral ground on this issue.

**Why do you use the term anti-racist education instead of multi-
cultural education?**

Partly because multicultural education often has come to mean
something that is quite superficial: the dances, the dress, the dialect,
the dinners. And it does so without focusing on what those expressions of culture mean: the values, the power relationships that shape
the culture.

I also use the term anti-racist education because a lot of multicultural education hasn't looked at discrimination. It has the view,
"People are different and isn't that nice," as opposed to looking at how
some people's differences are looked upon as deficits and disadvan-
tages. In anti-racist education, we attempt to look at — and change —
those things in school and society that prevent some differences from
being valued.

Often, whatever is white is treated as normal. So when teachers
choose literature that they say will deal with a universal theme or
story, like childhood, all the people in the stories are of European origin; it's basically white culture and civilization. That culture is different from others, but it doesn't get named as different. It gets named
as normal.

Anti-racist education helps us move that European perspective
over to the side to make room for other cultural perspectives that
must be included.

**What are some ways your perspective might manifest itself in a
kindergarten classroom, for example?**

It might manifest itself in something as basic as the kinds of toys and
games that you select. If all the toys and games reflect the dominant

culture and race and language, then that's what I call a monocultural classroom even if you have kids of different backgrounds in the class.

I have met some teachers who think that just because they have kids from different races and backgrounds, they have a multicultural classroom. Bodies of kids are not enough.

It also gets into issues such as: What kinds of pictures are up on the wall? What kinds of festivals are celebrated? What are the rules and expectations in the classroom in terms of what kinds of language are acceptable? What kinds of interactions are encouraged? How are the kids grouped? These are just some of the concrete ways in which a multicultural perspective affects a classroom.

How does one implement a multicultural or anti-racist education?

It usually happens in stages. Because there's a lot of resistance to change in schools, I don't think it's reasonable to expect to move straight from a monocultural school to a multiracial school.

First there is this surface stage in which people change a few expressions of culture in the school. They make welcome signs in several languages, and have a variety of foods and festivals. My problem is not that they start there. My concern is that they often stop there. Instead, what they have to do is move very quickly and steadily to

What can I do when a student makes a racist or sexist remark?

These kinds of remarks can catch us off guard, and the first instinct is often to respond strongly and cut off the speaker: "That kind of talk is not allowed here." Those of us in early childhood classes might also assume the kids are "too young" to really understand what they are saying.

Neither of these responses is adequate. Remember that curriculum is "everything that happens" at school. Your response or lack of response is just as much of a lesson as the morning math activity. Students will learn so much more if these issues are put on the table instead of under it.

Students also need to be explicitly taught the skills and

transform the entire curriculum. For example, when we say classical music, whose classical music are we talking about? European? Japanese? And what items are on the tests? Whose culture do they reflect? Who is getting equal access to knowledge in the school? Whose perspective is heard, whose is ignored?

The second stage is transitional and involves creating units of study. Teachers might develop a unit on Native Americans, or Native Canadians, or people of African background. And they have a whole unit that they study from one period to the next. But it's a separate unit and what remains intact is the main curriculum, the main menu. One of the ways to assess multicultural education in your school is to look at the school organization. Look at how much time you spend on which subjects. When you are in the second stage you usually have a two- or three-week unit on a group of people or an area that's been omitted in the main curriculum.

You're moving into the next stage of structural change when you have elements of that unit integrated into existing units. Ultimately, what is at the center of the curriculum gets changed in its prominence. For example: civilizations. Instead of just talking about Western civilization, you begin to draw on what we need to know about India, Africa, China. We also begin to ask different questions about why and

---

strategies that they will need to counteract racism and sexism in their lives. And developmentally, students should learn respect and how to take action against unfair behaviors or comments.

Responding properly is a multi-step process. You must consider not only who made the remark, but also the effect those words have on others in the classroom. Speak honestly about how the remark makes you feel. Stand up for the person or group that has been insulted. Give the other students the opportunity to respond as well. Beyond that, the whole issue of put-downs and name-calling should be an ongoing focus of the curriculum. These kinds of remarks can become a jumping-off point for meaningful classroom conversations.

— Rita Tenorio

what we are doing. Whose interest is it in that we study what we study? Why is it that certain kinds of knowledge get hidden? In mathematics, instead of studying statistics with sports and weather numbers, why not look at employment in light of ethnicity?

Then there is the social change stage, when the curriculum helps lead to changes outside of the school. We actually go out and change the nature of the community we live in. For example, kids might become involved in how the media portray people, and then start a letter-writing campaign about news that is negatively biased. Kids begin to see this as a responsibility, that they have to change the world.

I think about a group of elementary school kids who wrote to the manager of the store about the kinds of games and dolls that they had. That's a long way from having some dinner and dances that represent an "exotic" form of life.

In essence, in anti-racist education we use knowledge to empower people and to change their lives.

Teachers have limited money to buy new materials. How can they begin to incorporate a multicultural education even if they don't have a lot of money?

We do need money and it is a pattern to underfund anti-racist initiatives so that they fail. We must push for funding for new resources because some of the information we have is downright inaccurate. But if you have a perspective, which is really a set of questions that you ask about your life, and you have the kids ask, then you can begin to fill in the gaps.

Columbus is a good example. It turns the whole story on its head when you have the children try to find out what the people who were on this continent might have been thinking and doing and feeling when they were being "discovered," tricked, robbed, and murdered. You might not have that information on hand, because that kind of knowledge is deliberately suppressed. But if nothing else happens, at least you shift your teaching to recognize the native peoples as human beings, to look at things from their view.

There are other things you can do without new resources. You can include, in a sensitive way, children's backgrounds and life experiences. One way is through interviews with parents and community people, in which they can recount their own stories, especially their interactions with institutions like schools, hospitals, and employment agencies. These are things that often don't get heard.

I've seen schools invite grandparents to tell stories about their lives, and these stories get to be part of the curriculum later in the year. This allows excluded people, it allows humanity, back into the schools. One of the ways that discrimination works is that it treats some people's experiences, lives, and points of view as though they don't count, as though they are less valuable than other people's.

I know we need to look at materials. But we can also take some of the existing curriculum and ask kids questions about what is missing, and whose interest is being served when things are written in the way they are. Both teachers and students must alter that material.

How can a teacher who knows little about multiculturalism be expected to teach multiculturally?

I think the teachers need to have the time and encouragement to do some reading, and to see the necessity to do so. A lot has been written about multiculturalism. It's not like there's no information. If you want to get specific, a good place to start is back issues of the Bulletin of the Council on Interracial Books for Children.

You also have to look around at what people of color are saying about their lives, and draw from those sources. You can't truly teach this until you re-educate yourself from a multicultural perspective. But you can begin. It's an ongoing process.

Most of all, you have to get in touch with the fact that your current education has a cultural bias, that it is an exclusionary, racist bias and that it needs to be purged. A lot of times people say, "I just need to learn more about those other groups." And I say, "No, you need to look at how the dominant culture and biases affect your view of non-dominant groups in society." You don't have to fill your head with little details about what other cultural groups eat and dance. You need to take a look at your culture, what your idea of normal is, and realize it is quite limited and is in fact just reflecting a particular experience. You have to realize that what you recognize as universal is, quite often, exclusionary. To be really universal, you must begin to learn what Africans, Asians, Latin Americans, the aboriginal peoples, and all silenced groups of Americans have had to say about the topic.

> **VOICES FROM THE CLASSROOM**
>
> "THE STRUGGLE FOR quality education has been a centerpiece of freedom struggles throughout the United States, particularly for people of color. I think we have to understand that we have a special role to help continue that struggle."
>
> — Bob Peterson

How can one teach multiculturally without making white children feel guilty or threatened?

Perhaps a sense of being threatened or feeling guilty will occur. But I think it is possible to have kids move beyond that.

First of all, recognize that there have always been white people who have fought against racism and social injustice. White children can proudly identify with these people and join in that tradition of fighting for social justice.

Second, it is in their interest to be opening their minds and finding out how things really are. Otherwise, they will constantly have an incomplete picture of the human family.

The other thing is, if we don't make clear that some people benefit from racism, then we are being dishonest. What we have to do is

talk about how young people can use that from which they benefit to change the order of things so that more people will benefit.
If we say that we are all equally discriminated against on the
basis of racism, or sexism, that's not accurate. We don't need to
be caught up in the guilt of our benefit, but should use our privilege to help change things.

I remember a teacher telling me that after she listened to me
on the issue of racism, she felt ashamed of who she was. And I
remember wondering if her sense of self was founded on a sense
of superiority. Because if that's true, then she is going to feel
shaken. But if her sense of self is founded on working with people
of different colors to change things, then there is no need to feel
guilt or shame.

**Where does an anti-sexist perspective fit into a multicultural
perspective?**

In my experience, when you include racism as just another of the
-isms, it tends to get sidetracked or omitted. That's because people are sometimes uncomfortable with racism, although they may
be comfortable with class and gender issues. I like to put racism
in the foreground, and then include the others by example and
analysis.

I certainly believe that sexism and ageism and heterosexism
and class issues have to be taken up. But in my way of thinking I
don't list them under multicultural education.

For me, the emphasis is race. I've seen instances where
teachers have replaced a really sexist set of materials with non-
sexist materials, but the new resources included only white people. In my judgment, more has been done in the curriculum in
terms of sexism than in terms of racism.

Of course, we must continue to address sexism in all its
forms, no question about that. But we cannot give up on the fight
against racism either. As a black woman, both hurt my heart.

**How can a teacher combine the teaching of critical thinking
skills with a multicultural approach?**

I don't think there is any genuine multicultural approach without
a critical posture. But I am concerned when people say critical
thinking, because I am not sure what they mean. I think people

sometimes say critical thinking, and all they mean is thinking.

When I say critical thinking, I mean that we help youngsters ask questions about the social state of things, the social origins of things. What interests me are the kinds of questions one asks within the framework of teaching critical thinking skills.

For example, there are situations in which we have the kids thinking about the same old material from the same old Eurocentric point of view. Take the example of kids trying to resolve conflicts. In that process, we never challenge them to think about the unfair treatment, the racism, that may have led to the conflict in the first place, and that it is the unfairness that has to be changed if the conflict is really to be resolved.

What are some things to look for in choosing good literature and resources?

I encourage people to look for the voices of people who are frequently silenced, people we haven't heard from: people of color, women, poor people, working-class people, people with disabilities, and gays and lesbians.

I also think that you look for materials that invite kids to seek explanations beyond the information that is before them, materials that give back to people the ideas they have developed, the music they have composed, and all those things which have been stolen from them and attributed to other folks. Jazz and rap music are two examples that come to mind.

I encourage teachers to select materials that reflect people who are trying, and have tried, to change things to bring dignity to their lives: for example, Africans helping other Africans in the face of famine and war. This gives students a sense of empowerment and some strategies for making a difference in their lives. I encourage them to select materials that visually give a sense of the variety in the world.

Teachers also need to avoid materials that blame the victims of racism and other -isms.

In particular, I encourage them to look for materials that are relevant. And relevance has two points: not only where you are, but also where you want to go. In all of this we need to ask: What's the purpose? What are we trying to teach? What are we trying to develop?

One of the things I haven't talked about much is the outcome of the educational process. We need to ask ourselves: What is it that the student is experiencing as a result of their interaction with the materials? If the human beings we are working with aren't acquiring skills, knowledge, and attitudes that help them see themselves in a positive relationship with other human beings, then we have a problem.

Are we enabling African Americans and African Canadians, Native Americans and Native Canadians, in particular, to find and create a range of employment opportunities so they have financial resources and are able to make decisions about their lives? And does education encourage them to maintain healthy connections with their own communities and reject the racist images of them that are frequently portrayed in the media and elsewhere?

What can schools and school districts do to further multicultural education?

In the final analysis, multicultural or anti-racist education is about allowing educators to do the things they have wanted to do in the name of their profession: to broaden the horizons of the young people they teach, to give them skills to change a world in which the color of a person's skin defines their opportunities, where some human beings are treated as if they are just junior children.

Maybe teachers don't have this big vision all the time. But I think those are the things that a democratic society is supposed to be about.

When you look at the state of things in the United States and Canada, it's almost as if many parts of the society have given up on decency, doing the right thing and democracy in any serious way. I think that anti-racist education gives us an opportunity to try again.

But the conservative forces are certainly not going to allow this to happen without a battle. So we'd better get ready to fight. ■

"Brown Kids Can't Be In Our Club"

RAISING ISSUES OF RACE WITH YOUNG CHILDREN

I sat down one day with seven of the children in my first-grade class. It was early in the year and we were getting to know each other. We talked about how we were alike, how we were different. "Our skin is different," one of the children said. I asked everyone to put their hands together on the table, so we could see all the different colors.

One of my African-American students, LaRhonda, simply would not. Scowling, she slid her hands beneath the table top, unwilling to have her color compared to the others.

It was a reaction I had seen before. I teach at La Escuela Fratney, an ethnically diverse school in a racially mixed working-class Milwaukee neighborhood. My students typically include black kids, white kids, and Latinos. They have many things in common. Recess is their favorite time of day. Friendships are a priority. They want to "belong" to a group and they are very conscious of where they fit in a social sense.

And they all "know" that it is better to be light-skinned than dark-skinned.

BY RITA TENORIO

Even though my students have only six or seven years of life experience by the time they reach my classroom, the centuries-deep legacies of bias and racism in our country have already made an impact on their lives. I have seen fair-skinned children deliberately change places in a circle if African-American children sit down next to them. An English speaker won't play with a Latino child because, he says, "He talks funny." On the playground, a group of white girls won't let their darker-skinned peers join in their games, explaining matter-of-factly: "Brown kids can't be in our club."

As teachers, we have to acknowledge that we live in a racist society and that children typically mirror the attitudes of that society. Between the ages of 2 and 5, children not only become aware of racial differences, but begin to make judgments based on that awareness. They do this even though they may not be able to understand, in an intellectual way, the complexities of race and bias as issues.

> **VOICES FROM THE CLASSROOM**
>
> "RACISM IS REFLECTED IN a hierarchy in which beauty, intelligence, worth, and things associated with whiteness are at the top. The school is one site in which this hierarchical arrangement of skin power is confirmed daily. It is also a site where it can be undone."
>
> — Enid Lee, in "Anti-Racist Education: Pulling Together to Close the Gaps," in *Beyond Heroes and Holidays*

Teachers have a responsibility to recognize the influence of racism on themselves and their students. And we can help children learn the skills and strategies they will need to counteract it in their lives. At Fratney, our first-grade teams have put those ideas at the center of our practice.

Are They Too Young for This?

Many people would say that children at this age are too young to deal with these serious issues. I too had real questions at first about what was actually possible with young children. Can you have "real" conversations with 6-year-olds about power, privilege, and racism in our society? Can you make them aware of the effects that racism and injustice have in our lives? Can they really understand their role in the classroom community?

The answer to all of these questions is yes. Even very young children can explore and understand the attitudes they bring, and that their classmates bring, to school each day. They have real issues and opinions to share, and many, many questions of their own to ask. And in this way they can begin to challenge some of the assumptions that influence their behavior towards classmates who don't look or talk the same way they do.

Children at this age can explore rules and learn about collecting data, making inferences and forming conclusions. They can compare and contrast the experiences of people and think about what it means. They can, that is, if they are given the opportunity.

At Fratney, which serves 400 students from kindergarten through fifth grade, we discuss issues of social justice with all of our students. During the past several years, those of us teaching first grade have developed a series of activities and projects that help us to discuss issues of race and social justice in a meaningful, age-appropriate way.

We strive to build classroom community by learning about each other's lives and families. We ask our students to collect and share information about their families and ancestry. For example, we might talk about how they got their names; how their families came to live in Milwaukee; which holidays they celebrate and how. And at every step we help the children to explore the nature of racial and cultural differences and to overcome simplistic notions of "who's better" or who is "like us" and who isn't.

These activities include:

Me Pockets. This is always a class favorite. Each child takes home a letter-sized clear plastic sleeve, the kind used to display baseball cards. Students are asked to fill the pockets with photos, pictures, drawings, or anything else that will help us know more about them and the things that are important in their lives. The pockets are returned within a week and put into a three-ring binder that becomes the favorite classroom book to read and re-read.

The individual pockets reflect the cultural and socioeconomic diversity of the families. Some students put lots of photos or computer images in their pockets. Others cut pictures out of magazines or make drawings. Our experience is that every family is anxious to share in some way, and family members take time to help their children develop the project.

If someone doesn't bring their Me Pocket sheet back, the teachers step in to help them to find pictures or make the drawings they need to add their page to the binder.

I'm always amazed at how quickly the children learn the details about each other's lives from this project: who has a pet, who takes dance class, who likes to eat macaroni and cheese. The children know there are differences between them, but they also love to share the things that are alike.

"Look, Rachel has two brothers, just like me."

"I didn't know that Jamal's family likes to camp. We do too!"

Each of the teachers also completes a Me Pocket sheet. The students love looking at the picture of me as a first grader, seeing my husband and children, and learning that chocolate cake is my favorite food.

Partner Questions. Each day we take time to teach the social skills of communicating ideas with others and listening to another person's perspective. We use this time to "practice" those skills with role-playing activities and problem-solving situations they or we bring to the group. For example we might ask such questions as: What is the meanest thing anyone has ever said to you? Why do you think some people like to use put-downs? The children take a few minutes to talk about this with a partner. Afterwards some are willing to share with the whole group. We might then role play the situation as a group and look for ways to respond, such as speaking back to insults.

Remembering Someone Special. By the end of October, during the time of Halloween, Día de los Muertos, and All Souls' Day, we learn about how people remember their ancestors and others who have died or who are far away. We set up a table and encourage students to bring in pictures or artifacts to display. They bring a remarkable variety of things: jewelry, a trophy won by a departed relative, a postcard that person sent them, or perhaps the program from a funeral. And they bring many, many stories. Again, the teachers also participate and share stories of those who have gone before us. We get great responses from our students, and from their families.

Let's Talk About Skin. Another important conversation I have with my students focuses on the varieties of skin color we have in our group. Usually when we begin this discussion, some children are uncomfortable about saying "what they are" or describing the color of their skin. In particular, children with very dark skin — like LaRhonda, who would not even put her hands on the table — are often reluctant to join in. Meanwhile, the white kids often boast about

RESOURCES ON RACE FOR YOUNG CHILDREN

As the first-grade teachers at La Escuela Fratney have wrestled with presenting issues of race and culture to our young students in a meaningful way, we have found these resources helpful:

All the Colors of the Earth, by Sheila Hamanaka (New York: William Morrow and Co., 1994). 32 pp. $5.99.

A beautiful book that describes and celebrates the richness and variety of the many colors of skin. Hamanaka uses images of food, plants, and animals to connect the reader with the text. The message is clear: There is beauty and richness in every color. The children depicted in the book are very diverse and include children with special needs, mixed-race children, and children with albino characteristics.

All the Colors We Are: The Story of How We Get Our Skin Color, by Katie Kissinger (St. Paul, MN: Redleaf, 1997). 32 pp. $9.95.

This is a bilingual picture book — the text is presented in English and Spanish — about how people "get" their skin color. The text explores the basic facts about the roles that melanin, the sun, and ancestors play in making us different. The author uses photographs to explain the concepts in clear, child-friendly language that offers opportunities to explore this scientific concept with children.

Bein' with You This Way, by W. Nikola-Lisa (New York: Lee & Low, 1994). 32 pp. $6.95.

One of the favorite read-alouds in my classroom, this picture book is a joyful, rhythmic chant that celebrates diversity. Familiar, straightforward observations about size, hair texture, eye and skin color help the reader to dispel the notion of "normal" and recognize that we are all unique. Also available in a well-translated version.

The Colors of Us, by Karen Katz (New York: Henry Holt, 1999). 32 pp. $12.

When Lena decides to paint pictures of all of her friends she being "pink." Though we've never talked about this in class before, there is definitely a strong implication that it is better to be lighter. Many children are amazed that this topic is put out on the table for discussion. The looks in their eyes, their frequent reluctance to begin the discussion, tell me that this is a very personal topic.

As part of the lesson, we ask the students if they have ever heard anyone say something bad or mean about another person's skin color. The hands shoot up.

"My mom says that you can't trust black people."

"My sister won't talk to the Puerto Rican kids on the bus."

"Mara said that I couldn't play, that I was too black to be her friend."

---

is surprised to learn that brown is not just one color. In this picture book, Lena's mother takes her on a tour of the neighborhood to observe all the shades of "brown" skin. With new labels like "cinnamon," "chocolate," and "pizza crust," she begins to understand how four basic colors combine to make lots of variations. It serves as a great conversation starter on skin color.

We Can Work It Out: Conflict Resolution for Children, by Barbara Kay Polland (Berkeley, CA: Tricycle Press, 2000). 64 pp. $9.95.

A good resource to supplement the teaching of social skills. Through the use of photos and questions, Polland asks students and teachers to explore such issues as praise and criticism, jealousy, anger, and teasing. Lessons that start with the book can be extended in many ways with role plays, writing, and literature.

Whoever You Are, by Mem Fox (San Diego, CA: Voyager Books, 2001). 32 pp. $12.95.

A wonderful story that we use throughout the school year. With poetic language and mysterious, almost magical illustrations by Leslie Staub, this picture book tells the reader that "there are children all over the world just like you." Our students begin to see how all families experience the universality of love, joy, pain, and sadness.

— Rita Tenorio

They continue to raise their hands and this conversation goes on for a while. We talk about ways we've heard others use people's skin color to make fun of them or put them down. We talk about what to do in those situations.

As we continue to discuss issues of race, we teachers often introduce our personal experiences. I tell them about the first time I realized that black and white people were treated differently. I share my experience being one of the few Latinas in my school. And we try to ask questions that really intrigue the students, that invite them to try and look at things with a different perspective, to learn something new about the human experience and be open-minded to that idea: Did your ancestors come from a cold place or a warm place? Do people choose their color? Where do you get your skin color? Is it better to be one color than another? Lots of our conversations revolve around a story or a piece of literature. (See page 154 for suggested readings and classroom resources.)

With a little work, we can expand this discussion of skin color in ways that incorporate math lessons, map lessons, and other curricular areas. We've done surveys to see how many of our ancestors came from warm places or cold places. We ask children to interview their relatives to find out where the family came from. We create a bulletin board display that we use to compare and learn about the huge variety of places our students' relatives are from. We graph the data of whose family came from warm places, who from cold, who from both, or don't know.

Skin Color and Science. Our class discussions of skin color set the stage for lots of "scientific" observations.

For example, I bring in a large variety of paint chips from a local hardware store. The students love examining and sorting the many shades of beige and brown. It takes a while for them to find the one that is most like their own skin color.

In the story *The Colors of Us*, by Karen Katz, Lena learns from her mother that "brown" is a whole range of colors. Like the characters in the story, we take red and yellow and black and white paint and mix them in various combinations until we've each found the color of our own skin. Then we display our "research" as part of our science fair project.

In another exercise, inspired by Sheila Hamanaka's *All the Colors of the Earth*, students are asked to find words to describe the color of their skin, and to find something at home that matches their skin color. Then we display the pieces of wood and fabric, the little bags of cinnamon and coffee, the dolls and ceramic pieces that "match" us.

As we continue these explorations, dealing concretely with a topic that so many have never heard discussed in such a manner, students begin to see past society's labels. It is always amazing to children that friends who call themselves "black," for example, can actually have very light skin. Or that children who perceive themselves as "Puerto Rican" can be darker than some of the African-American children.

Writing About Our Colors. As children begin to understand the idea of internalizing another's point of view, they can apply that understanding by examining different ideas and alternatives to their own experiences. As they learn to express themselves through reading and writing, they can learn to challenge stereotypes and speak back to unfair behavior and comments.

Once students have had a chance to reflect on skin color, they write about it. Annie wrote: "I like my skin color. It is like peachy cream." James wrote: "My color is the same as my dad's. I think the new baby will have this color too." And Keila wrote: "When I was born, my color was brown skin and white skin mixed together."

When LaRhonda wrote about mixing the colors to match her skin, she said: "We put black, white, red, and yellow [together]. I like the color of my skin." How far she had come since the day she would not show us her hands.

Tackling Issues

These activities have an impact. Parents have spoken to us about the positive impression that these activities have made on the children. Many children have taken their first steps toward awareness of race.

They are not afraid to discuss it. They now have more ways in which to think about and describe themselves.

Yet these activities are no guarantee that children have internalized anti-racist ideas. So much depends on the other forces in their lives. We are still working on making these activities better: doing them sooner in the year, integrating them into other subjects, deepening the conversations, finding others' stories or activities to support them. Each year's group is different and their experiences and understandings must be incorporated. I learn something new every time. They challenge my consciousness too.

We rely on our schools to be the place for a multicultural, multiracial experience for our children. We want to believe that learning together will help our students to become more understanding and respectful of differences. Yet so often we do not address these issues head-on. It is unlikely that sensitivity and tolerance will develop, that children will bridge the gaps they bring to school from their earliest days, without specific instruction.

Personally, I want to see more than tolerance developed. I want children to see themselves as the future citizens of this city. I want them to gain the knowledge to be successful in this society. Beyond that, though, I want them to understand that they have the power to transform the society.

When students see connections between home and school, when lessons challenge them to look at the issue of race from multiple perspectives, we take the first steps in this process. ∎

All students' names have been changed.

Working Effectively With English Language Learners

A s communities across the United States are becoming more diverse, many new teachers are finding find that their responsibilities include teaching both academic content and language skills to English Language Learners.

There are many different types of bilingual ed/ESL program (see the box on page 160), and great differences can exist between programs that purport to serve students in similar ways.

Regardless of the type of program you're in, remember that it's your responsibility to deliver instruction to these students in a way that is understandable. That means organizing your teaching practice in a way that meets their needs, as well as "working the system" to ensure that these students are getting the services, such as extra support for taking tests, that they need.

BY BOB PETERSON AND KELLEY DAWSON SALAS

As a starting point, find out what kinds of services your school offers to support English Language Learners — and to support you as their classroom teacher. Ask your administrators, colleagues, or district bilingual/ESL office. Then do a little of your own research about English Language Learners and how their needs can best be served. (See the resource list on page 162 for some places to start.)

TYPES OF ESL
AND BILINGUAL PROGRAMS

English as a Second Language (ESL)

Emphasis is on learning and using English in the classroom and on preparing English Language Learners to function in "mainstream" English-language classrooms. English Language Learners may be placed in an English as a Second Language class, "sheltered English" classes, or they may participate in a pullout ESL class. ESL teachers may also support classroom teachers in their classrooms. Other languages typically are not used in ESL programs.

Transitional Bilingual Education

(Also referred to as "early exit bilingual education.")

Students' native language is used in classrooms to help students learn academic content while they are learning English. As soon as possible (usually two or three years), students are moved into instruction in English only. The goal is proficiency in English, not continuing to develop the student's native language skills.

Developmental Bilingual Education

(Also referred to as "maintenance bilingual education" or "late exit bilingual education.")

These programs develop and maintain proficiency in students' native language as well as English. Students entering developmental bilingual programs as kindergarteners are typically taught to read and write in their native language first, and then literacy skills are transferred to English. Once students function in both languages, they continue to learn language and content in both languages.

Dual Language Education

(Also referred to as "two-way bilingual" or "two-way immersion.")

These programs serve a mix of English Language Learners and native English-speaking students. They teach language and content in both English and in a target language (for example, Spanish, Japanese, etc.) The goal is for all students to become literate in both English and the target language, and to develop and maintain both languages.

Strategies for Improving Instruction
For English Language Learners

Speak slowly, audibly, and clearly in whatever language you use in the classroom. Avoid asking students in front of the whole class if they understand. Instead, ask students to volunteer to repeat the instructions in their own words, in English, or in the students' native language.

Prepare English Language Learners for challenging whole-class lessons ahead of time. In a small group, teach the second-language vocabulary that students will need to know. In addition to vocabulary, introduce the concepts that the whole class will be learning. Use materials that are geared for the specific group of English Language Learners (i.e., use materials in the students' home language and/or materials in English that are appropriate for the students' English reading level). That way when you teach the whole class lesson, English Language Learners have a head start because they've already had one comprehensible lesson on the topic.

Use lecture and verbal instruction as little as possible. Use visual cues such as posters, overhead pictures, slide shows, videos, and illustrated books. Use active methods of learning such as games, skits, songs, partner interviews, and structured conversation with class-mates. When necessary, explain concepts in the students' home language (have a colleague, parent volunteer, or student help if you are not able to do this). Finally, be prepared to spend additional time helping English Language Learners do the work. To keep things in perspective, try thinking about how your performance on the assignment would change if you were doing it in a language in which you were not yet fully proficient.

Use whole class instruction as little as possible. English Language Learners sometimes get lost and/or tune out during this kind of lesson. Whenever possible, work with small groups of children, or get students working on an assignment and circulate among them as they work.

In reading class, use literature — in English or the students' home language — that features the students' language/cultural groups. Give English Language Learners lots of attempts to be successful in a low-stress environment. Choral reading, echo reading, and partner reading all allow students to work on fluency and pronunciation without putting them on the spot. Rehearsing a sentence, paragraph, or page before reading it aloud to a group can help students to improve fluency one chunk of text at a time. Plays and skits provide a wonderful excuse to encourage students to practice the same lines over and over until they master them, and presenting a play or skit in their second language gives students a great sense of accomplishment.

RESOURCES FOR WORKING WITH ENGLISH LANGUAGE LEARNERS

Dual Language Instruction: A Handbook for Enriched Education, edited by Nancy Cloud, Fred Genesee, and Else Hamayan (Philadelphia: Heinle & Heinle, 2000).

Help! They Don't Speak English: Starter Kit for Primary Teachers, (Oneonta, NY: Eastern Stream Center on Resources and Training [ESCORT], 1998).

Learning and Not Learning English: Latino Students in American Schools, by Guadalupe Valdés (New York: Teachers College Press, 2001).

The Power of Two Languages: Literacy and Biliteracy for Spanish-Speaking Students, edited by Josefina Villamil Tinajero and Alma Flor Ada (New York: McMillan/McGraw Hill, 1993).

Dr. Jim Cummins' ESL and Second Language Learning Web, www.iteachilearn.com/cummins/index.htm
   This site offers details about Cummins' work researching second language acquisition and literacy development, and links to other web resources.

Stephen D. Krashen's Website, www.sdkrashen.com
   Information about Krashen's many informative articles and other writings about language learning.

Rethinking Schools Special Collection on Bilingual Education, www.rethinkingschools.org/special_reports/bilingual/resources.shtml
   This site provides a more in-depth listing of articles and resources for teachers working with English Language Learners.

Encourage students to maintain and develop their first language at school, at home, and in the community. Research shows that students learn English more effectively, and don't lag as far being their English-speaking classmates in other subject areas, when they do more academic work in their native language. And when students are pushed to learn English only, and aren't given the chance to continue learning their home language, they lose the opportunity to be bilingual, a skill that's increasingly valued in society.

Don't assume students have special education needs just because they're struggling academically. It could just be that they lack the language skills to successfully complete more academic work in English. At the same time, don't ignore potential special education needs either. Seek out resources in your school, district, and community to help you determine what is going on with a particular student.

Strategies for Becoming More Culturally Competent

If you do not yet speak the languages of the children you work with, start learning. Even if you do not master a student's language, learning a few words and courtesy phrases is a sign of respect and effort on your part. If you already speak your students' languages, congratulations! Continue to work at improving your skills.

Learn about the cultures of the children you teach. Listen to your students and show interest in their cultures while being careful not to put students on the spot or assume that they're experts on their cultures. Plan assignments that bring students' cultures, families, languages, and experiences front and center. Talk with colleagues, parents, and friends who share the students' backgrounds. Read, see movies, listen to music, travel to the students' home countries if possible. This is a lifelong process.

Find ways to communicate with parents in their first language unless they ask you to speak with them in English. For example, find out if an interpreter is needed and arrange for one ahead of time. ∎

Helping Students Deal with Anger

"**L**et me go! LET ME GO!!!" Michael's screams fill the entire second floor hallway. I imagine the noise bolting like lightning down the stairway, forcing its way through the double doors at the bottom and arriving abruptly in the principal's office.

Arms flail and one of Michael's fists connects with my teaching partner's ribs. I speak in what I hope is a soothing voice, although I know it is tinged with tension: "Michael, it's gonna be OK. We just need you to settle down a little bit first, Michael. As soon as you settle down we can let you go."

Michael was normally an outgoing, upbeat kid who was well-liked by his classmates and teachers. But from time to time he would just "drop out" of what the class was doing. Sometimes he would simply put his head down and withdraw. Sometimes he would start pushing and shoving his classmates. And sometimes he would escalate to a full-blown tantrum, which would grind the entire classroom to a halt.

This was one of those times.

BY
KELLEY
DAWSON
SALAS

By the time Michael was allowed to bring his hoarse voice and his third-grade body back into our classroom the next morning, I had decided that I needed to teach my young students some strategies on dealing with anger.

I was in my first year of teaching, trying to get my bearings. I was learning what kids were all about for the very first time. I was under the added pressure of going to school twice a week to meet the requirements of my alternative certification program. I simply didn't feel I had the time or the experience to help Michael respond to his emotions more appropriately.

Earlier in the year, after Michael's first few outbursts, I had pursued a different strategy and sought help for Michael from people outside of our classroom. I referred Michael for Collaborative Support Team action. "What can we do to find out what is behind Michael's angry behaviors?" I asked my principal and the members of the support team. "Is there some kind of anger management program he can participate in outside of the classroom? Can he receive counseling from the social worker or psychologist?" Michael did see the psychologist a few times after that. Both the social worker and I made calls to the family.

VOICES FROM THE CLASSROOM

"KIDS ARE NOT IN CONTACT with their feelings. They need to learn about themselves before they reach out and touch others. We can open our kids' eyes, help them to change."

— Floralba Vivas

But the flare-ups continued. In the classroom, nothing really changed. And of course I was not the only person in the classroom noticing Michael's behavior. The students also were keen observers. They saw how Michael put his head down on his desk and covered it up with his coat from time to time. They took a step backwards as he pushed a chair out of his way and into theirs, or hit another student on the playground and called it an accident. And several times, in situations when Michael exhibited angry behaviors, they had seen me give him a choice of "cooling down" and getting back to work or being asked to leave the classroom. More than once, they had witnessed him fly into a tantrum.

Other staff also were aware of Michael. During one episode, when there was a lull in Michael's screaming, I overheard the comments of a specialist who had stepped in to supervise my students: "We have to be real careful of Michael when he comes back to the classroom. We don't know what he'll do, do we?"

I didn't like the sound of that. As Michael's classroom teacher, I had observed that he sometimes had a difficult time handling his emotions and dealing with what I perceived as anger. I did not think about him as an angry person, and I was determined not to allow his peers or other staff members to categorize him as such. I felt this was especially important in a classroom where I, the teacher, was Anglo, almost all of the students were Latino, and Michael was one of three African-American boys. I did not want our classroom to be a place where students or staff were allowed to reinforce stereotypes that link anger with boys and men, especially African-American boys and men.

But the emotionally charged interactions that took place fairly regularly in our classroom indicated that something needed to change.

As I tried to help Michael through a long process of learning how to identify his feelings and emotions and respond constructively, I also went through an important learning process.

Lessons on Anger

I had to consider all the factors that contributed to our classroom dynamic. I had to examine my own beliefs, attitudes, and responses to Michael's behaviors. I had to consider how my actions as a white teacher of students of color affected Michael's emotions and responses. I had to try different approaches. These responsibilities weighed on me as I planned my course of action, and I continue to consider them as I reflect on what I did and what I might do differently next time.

For example, at the time I characterized Michael's outbursts as anger. Whether that is the appropriate emotional term, I am not sure; perhaps he was expressing frustration, or loneliness, or pain. I realize, in retrospect, that I used the term "anger" to describe strong emotional outbursts that may have had their origin in any number of emotions.

Teaching about anger immediately after a conflict with Michael didn't make sense. All eyes were on him. If I taught about anger during these moments, I would only be singling Michael out and escalating the problem. The rest of the students would pick up on my cue and would probably label him as an angry person. I might send an incorrect message that the only people who feel angry are those who act out the way Michael did.

Instead, I tried to plan a few simple lessons that would help all stu-

OTHER SOURCES OF ANGER

Our discussions around anger focused mostly on interpersonal relationships, and sought to understand what an individual can do when he/she feels angry. Looking back at this focus on individual interactions, I see that I missed an opportunity to guide students in an inquiry into other types of anger. I think it is important to help students understand that anger exists not only on an individual level, but can be related to societal issues of oppression and injustice.

This in turn could lead to a discussion of the role anger can play in the fight for social justice. As an activist for social justice, I use my anger at injustice to guide my own actions on a daily basis. Students can and should be aware that emotions often described as anger are not categorically "bad." Just as anger on an individual level can compel us to address a problem or make a change, the anger we feel when we witness injustice on a societal level should guide us toward changing unjust and oppressive systems. Rosa Parks comes quickly to mind as an example any third grader can understand.

— Kelley Dawson Salas

dents consider what anger is, what other emotions or experiences anger is linked to, and how we can respond. I drew upon my own personal experiences with anger and tantrums to put the lessons together.

The resources I used were minimal: I am sure there are much more extensive curricula on this topic. The important thing for me and my students was that these lessons helped us create a common framework for thinking about anger. Later I would refer to this framework in crisis moments or in interventions with Michael.

Safe Responses to Anger

I wanted my students to be able to identify the experiences and emotions that lead to what might be described as angry behaviors. I wanted ed them to recognize different responses to anger that they and others use. Most importantly, I wanted students to consider the choices we have for responding to strong emotions such as anger. I wanted them to recognize that when we are upset, we can either choose a course of action that is unsafe or unhealthy for ourselves and others, or we can choose a course of action that is safe and healthy.

I hoped this discussion would lead students not only to see that it is unacceptable to allow anger and strong emotions to explode in outbursts, but also to identify and practice safe responses when they feel angry.

I led three discussions with my students. First, we made a list of "things that make us angry." Students cited a great many sources of anger, from the trivial to the unjust. Some of their responses: "I get mad when I can't find the remote;" "when people treat me like I'm stupid;" "when we lose part of our recess;" and "when my mom hits me."

Second, we made a list of "things people do when they're mad." I encouraged the students to share examples of things they personally do when they're mad, and allowed them to share things they'd seen other people do. Many student responses were negative, hurtful or unsafe, such as: "I punch the nearest person;" "I hurt myself;" "I bang my own head against the wall;" "I kick or slam a door as hard as I can;" and "I yell at the person who's making me mad."

A couple of students offered up what I would categorize as "safe"

What should I do if I suspect a student is a victim of abuse?

It's very important that you know the procedure for your school or district. In most cases the answer is very clear: You are required by law to report suspicion of sexual or physical abuse.

Having said that, it's critical that these situations are handled sensitively and safely. Get some advice from the support staff (social workers, psychologists, counselors) or community resource people who work with your students.

If you make a report, ask for assurances you will not be identified as the reporter to the suspected abuser.

— Rita Tenorio

responses to anger: "I go for a bike ride to blow off steam;" "I go in my room and read until I'm not mad anymore;" "I talk to my mom about what's making me mad." I asked the students: "Can you think of any other things like that, things that would help you to cool down or solve the problem?"

They suggested a few more: "You could talk to an adult you trust;" "go for a walk or go outside and play;" "tell the person who's making you mad how you feel."

Finally, we made a large poster to hang in the classroom that showed different responses to anger. The students each made their own copy of the poster for their own use. In the center, the question "What can you do when you feel angry?" prompted kids to remember the responses we had brainstormed in the previous activity. The top half of the poster was reserved for writing in safe or healthy responses to anger, while the bottom half was labeled "unsafe/scary." While completing this activity, we had a chance to discuss the idea that each person must make a choice when angry about what course of action to take. I again reminded the students that some responses to anger are safe and some are not.

By helping students see the connection between their responses to anger and adults' responses, I tried to encourage them to understand that each of us has a lifelong responsibility to resolve anger appropriately and safely.

Rather than just telling students to respond "safely" to a situation that makes them mad, they need to be taught to consider the source of their anger and to develop a response that is not only safe but also effective. Routine bickering with a sibling might be effectively solved by some time apart, for example, while a series of name-calling incidents or physical bullying by a classmate will not be resolved just by walking away one more time. Students should be encouraged to see the difference between a response which simply helps them blow off steam, and one that actively seeks to address the cause of their anger and solve the problem.

Michael Joins In

Several complexities surfaced in our discussions. Michael, who in addition to his tantrums had also been known to crumple his papers in frustration, asked about how to classify these kinds of actions. "Is it safe to crumple up your paper? You're not hurting anyone if you do that."

What do I do when I realize I've made a mistake with a child?

Since you are a person and not some trained robot, chances are that you will make mistakes, such as losing your cool or saying something that you really did not mean to say to a student. We really should try to keep these to a minimum, but when you do make a mistake it is important to acknowledge your error publicly.

One time, for example, I made a comment to a student in front of our class and as soon as I said it, I knew I shouldn't have. I should have been able to control my anger, but I didn't. It was right before lunch, so I had time to consider what I would say upon the students' return to the classroom.

I didn't make a big dramatic scene, but I did apologize in front of everyone. I explained that I had lost my temper. I said that I expected more of the student and his behavior, but more of myself, too. I asked, in front of his peers, if he would accept my apology. He did and we moved on.

It wasn't easy admitting I was wrong in front of 27 kids, but I thought it was important for them to see me as human. It also helped with discipline. When I later had to ask a student to apologize to another for lack of respect of property, feelings, or personal space, the students had already seen me do the same. And they had seen one of their classmates accept an apology rather than continue a cycle of anger and revenge. More often than not, my students were willing to patch things up right there.

— Stephanie Walters

It depends on whether the mistake was made in public and whether it embarrassed or humiliated the student. If you messed up in public in a way that was hurtful to a student, then you have to try to correct it in public — to the extent possible. For example, as a new teacher you will likely struggle with main-

"Well, let's think about that one," I responded. "It might not be physically dangerous to anyone, but is it hurting you in any way? Does it hurt you when you put your head down for hours and decide not to learn or do your work?" My hope was that Michael would slowly come to realize that he was hurting himself with some of his behaviors.

Michael participated during these sessions just as any other student. I did not single him out or use him as an example. In fact, I tried hard not to allow myself or the other students to refer to his behavior in our discussions. I did keep a close eye on him, and noticed that he participated actively. His brainstorming worksheets also gave me an idea of some of the things that made him angry, and some of his usual responses to anger at school and at home. This was important to my work with Michael because it allowed me to think about possible causes of his behaviors without having to do it in a moment of crisis, and without making him feel like he was being singled out.

"Why Do Adults Do It?"

I should make clear that I did not assume or suspect that Michael was dealing with anger or violence in his own family. Rather, I planned this lesson in order to address the students' concerns, and to give students a clear message that adults are responsible for making safe choices when faced with anger.

During our talks about anger, students' questions provided a springboard to an additional discussion that could have turned into a whole unit of its own. As we looked together at the abundance of

taining classroom decorum. Depending on the students, the time of year, the time of day, and how much sleep you've had, you may come down on a student in an unfair way. Apologies can be important, and many students will respect a teacher who can admit that he/she made a mistake. It also may go a long way toward repairing a relationship with a member of your class.

Remember, everything you do in class is education, so how you treat people in public is always more than "classroom management." It's also a vital piece of the curriculum.

— Bill Bigelow

unsafe or violent responses to anger, a few students began to ask: "If we're not supposed to throw tantrums, why do so many adults do it?"

They're right, I thought. How can I tell them that they should choose safe responses to anger when so many adults choose verbal outbursts or even physical violence? How and when can we hold adults responsible for their angry behaviors? I allowed my teaching to take a brief detour in pursuit of an answer to these important questions.

I designed a lesson in which I talked about my own experiences with adults and anger, and shared a poem about a parent's angry outbursts. Together we discussed a few key concepts about adult anger and tantrums. We discussed the fact that adults, just like kids, must make choices about how to act when they are angry. Some adults make poor choices, I said.

I also wanted to make sure that my students didn't internalize feelings of guilt over an adult's anger, as if they were somehow to blame for the outburst. I pointed out that it is not a child's fault if an adult they know responds to anger in a way that hurts others. I referred back to a previous unit we had done on human rights and asserted that as human beings, we have a right to live free from the threat of angry outbursts and violence. We agreed that it is important for us to talk with someone we trust if someone is threatening that right. Adults can change their behaviors, and may need help to do so.

These affirmations provided a very basic introduction which could have easily turned into a much more profound examination of anger and violence in families — our discussion only scratched the surface.

Some Changes, Some Progress

The school year went on. Michael did not miraculously change overnight, but he did make some changes, and so did I. In situations where he resorted to angry behaviors, we had a language in which to talk about his feelings and his choices for responding to them. I also had developed more sensible and effective strategies for helping Michael through tough times. Many times, I said to him, "It's clear to me that you're feeling frustrated or angry. Are you choosing to deal with your feelings in a safe way?"

Later in the year when Michael was angry, he was no longer as likely to say to me: "Look what you made me do." He knew I would respond by saying, "You choose what you do."

Things got easier. The cooling-down periods got shorter. He seemed to be taking more responsibility for his actions and developing some strategies for what to do when he felt frustrated or angry.

For my part, I tried to become more flexible and to stop trying to force Michael to respond exactly as I wanted him to when he felt angry. I always tried to get to what triggered his discontent and to acknowledge his feelings.

Perhaps most importantly, I learned not to touch Michael while he was angry, or to try to move him physically. I had seen that that simply did not work.

I was relieved that we had found a somewhat workable solution to Michael's behavior in our classroom. Part of me continued to wonder whether there were circumstances in Michael's life that were causing anger and frustration to build up. I kept working with his family and advocating with school support staff for additional help for him. I talked with him often about his feelings and tried to be alert to signs of a more serious problem without making unfounded assumptions.

Michael and I worked together for a year and I think each one of us made some progress. As I struggled to become an effective teacher in my first year on the job, I was willing to learn from anyone who wanted to teach. Michael proved to have a lot of lessons in store for me. How little I would have learned had I simply written him off.

For his part, Michael could have just as easily turned his back on me. I am thankful to him for giving me a chance to be his teacher and to learn from him. ■

The Challenge of Classroom Discipline

O ne of the most daunting challenges for teachers — new and veteran alike — is classroom discipline. Each new class of students brings a new set of difficulties and possibilities, whether it's your first year of teaching or your twenty-first.

Education author Alfie Kohn has written that given all the pressures on teachers, there's a tendency to narrowly frame this issue in terms of compliance, seeing the key question as, "How can I get my kids to obey?" Other questions, however, frame the issue in a more fruitful way:

- What are the needs of the kids?
- How might we meet those needs?
- How can we build a community of serious learners who respect one another?

To frame one's approach to discipline using these questions, as Kohn suggests, is more challenging, but ultimately more successful and positive for students and teacher alike.

BY
BOB
PETERSON

Most students have been conditioned to expect that they need to behave and be serious learners only if there are external rewards and punishments. Schools have increasingly resorted to these "external" approaches to discipline as part of an omnipresent textbook-centered and test-driven curriculum that is disconnected from students' lives and offers little inspiration. Boredom and academic frustration are fertile ground on which students' preexisting social and emotional problems take root and blossom.

For a teacher to meet students' needs and build a community of learners, a number of things have to happen. Solid teacher-student and student-teacher relationships must be built. Students need to be involved in conversations about creating a community and have the chance to practice the necessary skills. They need to work regularly with partners and in groups and reflect on that work. They need a challenging curriculum, connected to their lives, that involves not only listening but doing. They need to understand that it is OK to make mistakes, that learning involves more than getting the "right" answer. They need to participate in making decisions. And finally, they need to feel

VOICES FROM THE CLASSROOM

"YOU ABSOLUTELY CANNOT teach anything until you build a community in the classroom — until they all know each other's names, until they all know how to get along with each other."

— Sara Schneider Cruz

that the classroom atmosphere engenders trusting relations between teacher and students and among students themselves.

Teachers need to be clear about what is and what is not within the purview of student decision-making — whether it's choosing what they write, read, and study; deciding the nature of their collaborative projects; or helping establish the classroom's procedures. Teachers also need to figure out, through practice, what "noise" and activity level they are comfortable with in the classroom, how they will deal with a severely disruptive student, and how they will build strong ties with parents.

On the macro level, teachers need and deserve a schoolwide environment in which all staff and students are treated respectfully, where supportive services are available for students with significant difficulties, and where staff have the time to collaboratively discuss discipline and curricular issues.

By now you might be thinking, "These guidelines are all fine and good, but what do I actually do to make them a reality?"

The first thing to realize is that taking a non-punitive approach to discipline is not easy. There is no one quick fix, chart, or schema that will solve all or even most of your discipline problems. The human mind and emotions are much more complex than even the most sophisticated discipline plan, and as teachers we are dealing with dozens of minds simultaneously. Some students may have spent years distrusting adults or their classmates. To help students learn the emotional and social skills necessary to work in crowded classroom settings is a monumental challenge.

Should I try to be a friend to my students?
This is a complicated question. The short answer is no. They've got friends; you've got friends. True friendship requires equality, and in many respects you and your students are not equals. You are a leader, you are a guide, you are a mentor, you are an evaluator.

I've seen new teachers so desperate to be liked by their students that they cannot maintain discipline in the classroom, are not academically rigorous, and end up doing a great disservice to students. However, the "don't smile until Christmas" advice is also misplaced.

At its core, teaching is about relationships, and unless you have a solid, respectful, supportive relationship with your students, you won't be able to teach effectively and students won't be able to learn effectively.

Also, frankly, if you're not having fun teaching, then you won't last as a teacher. You need to create activities in which you and the students are having a good time. You need to create activities in which you are able to appreciate the best qualities of the students. This is for them, but it's also for you. But working to build a playful, joyful, respectful, hardworking classroom is different from being the students' "friend."

— Bill Bigelow

And speaking as a veteran teacher I can tell you that no matter how long you teach, you will still struggle with discipline issues, making progress on some days, only to feel that progress evaporate on other days.

Beyond Rewards and Punishment

Discipline should not be seen as synonymous with punishment; good behavior not equivalent to rewards and incentives. While aspects of reward and punishment may appear in a classroom discipline plan, they should not be its foundation.

Instead, a sound discipline plan is centered on building trusting relationships and a sense of community through conversation, modeling, problem-solving, clear rules, consistency, and perseverance. Substantive conversation should start on the first day of school and be woven throughout the school day and year.

In my fifth-grade classroom I start the year with the question: "What would you like this class to be like?" With the help of a few probing questions from me, we discuss what the students would like to study and what they'd like the social relations in the class to be like.

Early in the year I explain how laws and rules are made by the varying levels of government, the school board, the school itself, and the classroom teacher. I let kids know that school rules are set by educators experienced in running a school, and that occasionally such rules are modified when people (students, parents, or teachers) raise questions or objections. If they disagree with rules made outside of the classroom, I say, they should voice their concerns.

I explain that since I respect their ideas, I want them to be involved in deciding many classroom procedures. I hold authority in my classroom, I tell them, and my willingness to agree to their proposals is dependent on two things: the soundness of their ideas and their ability as a group to show that they are responsible enough to assume decision-making power.

Things don't always go smoothly. One year while discussing classroom rules the kids were adamant that anybody who broke a rule should sit in a corner with a dunce cap on his/her head. I refused on the grounds that it was humiliating. Eventually we worked out other consequences, including time-outs and loss of a privilege such as lunch recess.

Another year students came up with the idea of creating a class "promise" about what they wanted in the classroom. After brainstorming as a whole group a committee of four children drafted the following during recess:

"On our honor we promise to help make a peaceful classroom. We promise to be responsible. We won't bully people or call names, but treat people nicely with kindness. We won't judge people for how they look but for what's inside. We won't have racism or sexism in our class. We promise to try our best in everything and to be serious learners. We promise to make our class peaceful and fun."

The committee presented the statement to the entire class. Everyone signed it except two boys who, despite the encouragement of their classmates, refused. (One boy soon transferred out of the school for unrelated reasons, while the other remained in the classroom that year, generally behaving himself but appreciating the notoriety his refusal to sign gave him.) Throughout the year I referred back to the statement to remind students what it takes to create a classroom of serious learners.

Sometimes my class discussions take place in the course of the normal school day, but often they are during class meetings: We push the desks back, sit in a circle on the floor, and use a "talking stick," allowing only the holder of the stick to speak. At the beginning of the school year I hold meetings daily, but they usually evolve to once or twice a week. Some elementary teachers hold class meetings to start the day when homework is collected, announcements are made, and substantive discussions are held. Middle and high school teachers hold them less frequently, but find that collective discussion and reflection is essential to building a healthy environment for classes that meet only 48 minutes a day.

Becoming Fluent in Positive Behaviors

One of the main goals of the class meetings and our discussions is to get the students to internalize the notion that they are a community of serious learners who respect each other. Teachers need to help each student define — or redefine — his/her social identity as an achiever, and they need to help students practice becoming fluent in acting out positive behaviors.

Thus, in addition to discussions envisioning what the class should look like, modeling specific behaviors and role-playing situations are crucial to successful classroom discipline. One way to get students to think about what a community of learners looks like during different activities is to use a "T-chart." The teacher draws a big "T" on the chalkboard and titles the left side "looks like" and the right side "sounds like." Kids brainstorm what an outside visitor would see and hear during certain activities. For example, when we make a T-chart about how to conduct a class discussion, students list things like "one person talking" on the left side and "kids looking at the speaker" and "children with their hands raised" on the right side.

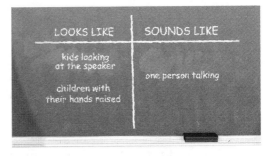

Later we make a copy of the T-chart and hang it on the wall; this helps most children remember what is appropriate behavior for different activities.

Modeling appropriate behavior is essential in building a classroom of learners. This should include everything from how to work with a partner (how to introduce yourself, how to decide what to focus on, what to do if a partner is becoming distracted, what to do when there is a disagreement, etc.), to working in groups, to making transitions between subject areas. A teacher shouldn't assume that once an activity is modeled, it's smooth sailing for the year. Regular modeling is important, as is class discussion of the rough spots in a partnering or group activity.

But even with these reminder activities, things don't always work out. For example, just when I think the students have developed the habit of working in partners or small groups without complaining about who they are with, a student will throw a fit about not wanting to work with "so and so," making me question how effective my teaching is.

By role-playing different situations, students can problem-solve how best to handle conflicts like these. I teach students how to give "I messages": "I feel (state the feeling) when you do (state the specific behavior) because it (state the effects on you)." Sometimes we add the phrase "So please...."

I also teach students to use "self talk" as one technique to manage their anger or help them self-monitor their activities. Sometimes as a class we will address a classwide problem — such as a particular rash of name-calling, or a continual lack of pencils. We use a problem-solving model in which we:

- Identify the problem.
- Discuss why the problem exists.
- Brainstorm solutions.
- Discuss the positive and negative of each proposed solution.
- Choose one of the proposed solutions.
- Decide how the class will know if it is successful.

For example, a problem as simple (and as frustrating) as students always needing to get up to sharpen their pencils was solved after group discussion: I bought some extra pencils and placed two containers, labeled "sharp pencils" and "dull pencils," in the back of the room. Students needing a sharp pencil could just exchange a dull pencil for a sharp one, without the disruptive act of sharpening their pencil during class time. At the end of the day a student volunteer sharpens all the dull pencils.

One-on-One

Sometimes I have problem-solving activities on the classroom level, but equally important are problem-solving conversations between me, as the teacher, and an individual student who is having difficulty.

I use a system in which each child's name is on a clothespin that is clipped to a rope that hangs down on the wall in the front of the room. The students put their names up on the top section of the rope when they enter (this helps with attendance). If a student misbehaves his/her name is "lowered" to the yellow "reminder" section. A second misbehavior and the student's pin is put in the "reflection" section, which means the student has to write about what difficulties he/she is having being part of a community of learners. The student must also have a conference with the teacher about the problem.

A third incident and the pin is lowered to the "response" section and parent contact is made through a note or call home. Another problem, and the pin is placed in the "removed" section, which means the student goes to another classroom or to the office.

The focus at of this system is not punishment, but reminders of what is appropriate behavior, conversation, reflection, and planning between the teacher and student (and eventually the adult in the student's life) about what can be done differently. Through this process, trust is built between the student and teacher, even in the most difficult situations. At the end of the day I note on a class list who has had their pin lowered, so that over time I can see patterns and, if necessary, take more drastic action like requesting a face-to-face parent conference or help from the school psychologist.

Know Your Limits, Set Your Standards

For new teachers, a crucial part of any such plan is to be aware of what their limits and standards are. When is it appropriate for students to sharpen their pencils, leave to go to the bathroom, or discuss something with a classmate? What noise level is acceptable during writing workshop or a cooperative math activity? Once a teacher is clear in his/her own mind, it's much easier to model the behavior and expect students to follow it.

Noise level is always an issue. Here again, discussion about the issue is an important first step. Once students are reminded why different levels of noise and activity are appropriate at different times, I use simple signs to help remind students. I have a large sign with "Silent Time" on one side, and "Soft-Spoken Time" on another that I flip back and forth when

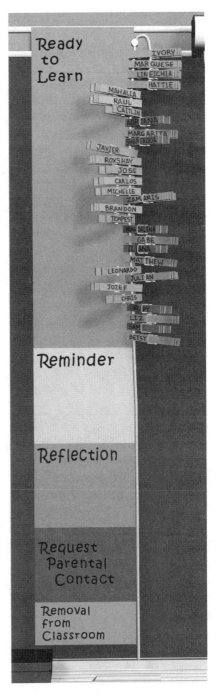

appropriate. I have also used a "Volume Control" sign with numbers 0 through 5. I tell students what the volume should be: 0 during a presentation, maybe a 2 during cooperative group time, or higher during a class snack. It they get too loud I tell them, "You're at volume 4 and it has to be lowered." Or when moving from a transition period to a lesson I tell them to "mute the volume" — something that all TV-saturated students seem to understand.

Another technique for helping with noise and attention is the development of classroom rituals so that students anticipate certain things. For example, I always start my day off with a song of the week (see "The Power of Songs in the Classroom" on page 133). I also have students place books for silent reading on their desks before lunch, so that they don't have to waste time right after lunch finding them. Before I share a story or read a chapter book aloud, I light a candle or hang a special weaving in the front of the room as a signal, and students usually quiet down and get ready for that activity.

Classroom organization is another essential ingredient in building a community of learners. Some years I have the desks in my class

Q/A

How do I prepare for a substitute teacher?
Don't ever assume that the person who will take your class will come prepared. Sometimes that happens. Lots of times it doesn't. Put together a folder that the substitute can find easily. Include basics like a class list and seating chart, procedures for the day, duties that the sub may have to cover for you, and bus lists and dismissal information so no one gets lost when school lets out.

And include worksheets for your kids to do. Sometimes the work that a substitute plans to give your students will be in direct conflict with the way you've been teaching. Don't take the chance of your kids spending the day coloring worksheets about holidays, copying paragraphs to practice penmanship, or playing Hangman. Instead, make sure that the worksheets or games are ones that will connect to your students and the work you do in your classroom.

arranged in five groups of six each, which serve as "base groups." I rearrange the base groups when I feel it's time for a change, always taking into account language dominance, race, gender, and special needs, creating heterogeneous groups to guard against those subtle forms of elementary school "tracking." (See "Getting Your Classroom Together" on page 26 for a more thorough discussion of classroom arrangements.)

Throughout the day children might work in a variety of partner or cooperative learning groups, but their base group remains the same. In each group different students have responsibilities, varying from collecting homework and passing out papers to making sure everyone in the group is prepared and ready to learn.

Sometimes I allow the group that is the best prepared to start a new activity, to help in a dramatization, or to be the helpers for that lesson. This provides incentive for the groups to get even the most recalcitrant students to join in with classroom activities. In this way, many of the classroom management tasks are taken on by the students, creating a sense of collective responsibility. (Arranging the stu-

---

Find a colleague who will agree to check in with a sub on the days you are gone and vice-versa. The colleague can alert the sub to specific information that might be needed that day.

As wonderful as your students might behave for you on a daily basis, know that they will probably give the substitute a hard time. Having things prepared for them that they like to do, that will challenge them a bit, will make their day without you at least somewhat productive.

It's important that you find out later how the day with the sub went. Some schools have the secretary ask subs to complete a form before they leave. Find out what the students thought too. Take note of subs who do a good job and keep their names for future reference. Likewise, alert your principal to those substitute teachers you wouldn't want to use again.

— Rita Tenorio

dents' desks in these base groups also has the added advantage of freeing up classroom space for dramatizations or classroom meetings where kids sit on the floor.)

Challenging Students

Even with all these various techniques and community-building activities — and even after years of teaching experience — I still encounter students from time to time who are very disruptive, who are so challenging that they make me question many of the positive approaches toward classroom management.

But when confronted with such students, I've never had success adopting a more traditional, repressive, or threatening approach. To the degree I slide down that slippery slope, the problem almost always gets worse — maybe not in the short term, but certainly over the long haul. My experience has been that the best way to approach these extremely difficult students is to enlist as much help as one can — from the parents, fellow teachers, your union representative, the administrators, and the social worker or psychologist. Seek out the help and demand it. If I am having difficulty, it's likely that others are as well. And since we are operating as a school community, it's also other peoples' responsibility to help solve the problem — especially the administration's.

A well-organized class that is respectful and involves the students in some decision-making is a prerequisite for successful learning. Cooperative organization and student involvement alone won't build a community of learners, but they are essential building blocks in its foundation. ■

Some of the ideas in this article are adapted from the book *Learning to Trust: Transforming Difficult Elementary Classrooms Through Developmental Discipline,* by Marilyn Watson with Laura Ecken (San Francisco: Jossey-Bass, 2003).

The Best Discipline
Is Good Curriculum

During my first year of teaching, I tried everything to get my students to behave. Behavior charts, individual plans. Class incentives, class consequences. Tricks, threats. Rewards, punishments. Strict attitude, friendly attitude. Yelling, reasoning, sweet-talking, pleading for sympathy.

One day, I wrote the word "celebration" on the board and promised the class they could have a party if they behaved for the whole day. I crossed each letter off one by one. By noon we all knew they'd never make it. In short, I was desperate.

Discipline is an exhausting part of the job that never really goes away. The message that most of us get is that to be a good teacher, you must first be a good disciplinarian. You must control your students' behavior. Only then, when your classroom is under control, can you begin to teach. I disagree.

No teacher has to wait until the students are "under control" to start teaching them worthwhile stuff. It's actually the other way around. Over and over again, I have found that the moment I start to teach interesting, engaging content, I experience immediate relief in the area of discipline.

BY
KELLEY
DAWSON
SALAS

During my first year, my classroom was pret-

185

How can I prepare my students for a field trip?

First, remember that many families simply can't afford extra fees for field trips. Try to find free or inexpensive activities. One of my schools was right on a major university campus, so there were a lot of low-cost cultural events available. I also sought out trips that were significantly discounted to students through arrangements with our school district.

Second, have a clear idea of what you expect your students to accomplish on the trip. I've worked with colleagues who would create elaborate learning packets for students to complete on field trips. Then they would give the students grades and even test them on the material.

I view field trips in a much different light. I told my students to be aware that people are watching them. I told them, "Some people will have a negative opinion of you and low expectations of your behavior." We discussed whether it's right for others to judge them like that, and of course they said no. So I posed the question: "How will we make sure that people see us differently?"

The first time I asked this question, one student raised her hand and replied, "Be good."

"OK, fine, but what does it mean to be good?" I responded.

That was a more difficult question; kids don't always know what we want, so they say "be good" as their catchall answer.

We discussed specific appropriate behavior before each field trip. For example, if we were going to see a play, there should be plenty of applause for the actors, no talking during the performance, no kicking the seat in front of you, and no screaming when they dim the lights!

For practice, in class before a trip I would ask students to demonstrate "good" and "not-so-good" behavior. Once in a while there would be a slip-up on a trip, but we would discuss it and figure out how the students could improve their behavior. And almost every time they did improve.

— Stephanie Walters

ty wild. (Don't hold it against me; I know you've been there!) But it made sense to me that my students acted the way they did. I was a brand-new teacher, totally inexperienced. My students wanted more than I could offer them, and they were bored and confused much of the time. I didn't really see how forcing them to behave would change that.

It took some time, but eventually I quit working so hard at controlling my students' behavior and started focusing on my own: What was I teaching? What methods was I using? What was I doing to engage, to teach students so that they would not be bored and disruptive?

I looked at what I was doing in social studies: plodding through a textbook that was inaccurate, boring, and disconnected from my students' lives. I decided to teach some lessons about the Civil Rights Movement, and to have the class write and perform a play about the Montgomery bus boycott. It was an extremely rough first attempt at writing and teaching my own curriculum, but for our purposes, it worked. I was engaged, the students were engaged, and we all spent a lot less time dealing with discipline.

In my subsequent years of teaching, I've had similar experiences. Every time there's a slump in my teaching — yes, even though I work hard, it happens — kids get bored (I get bored, for that matter) and discipline gets hairy. It's like a rumbling that slowly turns to a roar and ultimately demands action: If you don't plan some good curriculum, things are really going to get out of control here.

Of course, it's important to have rules and consequences, and to apply them consistently while teaching interesting content. I find it works well to remind kids frequently why an ordered environment helps them learn, to show them how rules and consequences help create a classroom where real learning can happen. Also, when

VOICES FROM THE CLASSROOM

EQUITY AND JUSTICE MUST come to life in your classroom. It is in your classroom that students will experience the world, a world that opens possibilities for their developing hearts and minds. Always do what is in the best interest of your students. You are preparing them for a future that we can only imagine. Don't shortchange them because of external pressures.

— Kathy Swope

VOICES
FROM THE
CLASSROOM

"SET CLEAR, HIGH EXPECTA-tions for all students. Don't feel sorry for kids. They don't need your pity; they need you to give them tools and knowledge to navigate the education system. Don't excuse them from homework or higher level skills or more challenging work. They need clear and consistent high expectations."

— Linda Christensen

I'm teaching something I really believe is worth my students' time, I feel more authority to demand a high standard of behavior.

Even the best curriculum can't magically solve all behavior issues. Our society creates a lot of pressures and problems for kids, and they often bring these to school. Students witness violence, live in poverty, struggle to help hard-working parents, and watch a ton of TV, much of it inappropriate. Some students have serious problems that will not go away without specific intervention. It may help to work with the school psychologist, social worker, or administrators in these cases. Teachers can also push for schoolwide preventive programs like anti-bullying, anger management, or peer mediation. These can have a great impact on behavior.

I'm now in my fourth year of teaching, and I'm still struggling to create all the curriculum I need to motivate and engage my fourth graders for six hours a day. Whenever I feel overwhelmed by the size of that task, I try to remind myself to think small: I go back to my first year and remember that back then, even one good lesson was sometimes enough to tip the scales from boring, intolerable, and out of control to what I could at least call "manageable."

Each year, I am building upon those lessons and offering better and better curriculum to my students. I know discipline issues will never completely disappear from my classroom. But I also know good curriculum goes a long way toward making my classroom run smoothly. And engaging curriculum is more than just a fix for behavior headaches. It can also get kids to think deeply, care about our world, and help them learn to make positive changes.

As a bonus, I feel less foolish now that I don't have to stand at the front of the class and take away my students' celebration one letter at a time. ∎

CHAPTER FOUR

Dealing with the World Beyond Your Classroom

Teaching in the Undertow

RESISTING THE PULL
OF SCHOOLING-AS-USUAL

As a 7-year-old, I was amazed by the ocean. I remember being awed as I looked out at the vastness of the water off the South Carolina coast. And I recall the cautionary words my mother used each time I tried to wade in deeper than my waist: "Be careful of the undertow."

According to my mom, the undertow was an invisible current beneath the ocean's surface that, if you weren't careful, could pull you down the coastline or out to sea before you knew what was happening. It tugged you along almost imperceptibly, she said, so you had to consciously keep your bearings: Pick a recognizable landmark and don't lose sight of it.

I could have used her advice when I began teaching seventh and eighth grade on Chicago's south side two decades later. I went in with no formal preparation or credentials, and as a white male transplanted from the South, I was an outsider to my students in many ways. My approach at the time grew out of what made sense to me. I thought classrooms should be active spaces where kids had regular opportunities to do and make things. I thought students should be encouraged to express themselves creatively. I thought their voices should be not only heard, but valued. I believed

BY
GREGORY
MICHIE

kids should feel a connection between what they studied in school and their lives outside school. And I felt they should be pushed to think critically about the world around them.

Most of all I recognized that a meaningful, quality education was crucial for the young people I would be teaching, whose communities had been largely neglected and abandoned by those in power.

But having beliefs or guiding principles is one thing. Figuring out how to put them into practice, I learned, is another matter altogether, especially if you're teaching at a struggling urban school where the "pedagogy of poverty," as Martin Haberman calls it — characterized by "constant teacher direction and student compliance" — is in widespread use.

In that sort of environment, it's easy to lose your footing as a novice teacher, to begin to drift from your anchorage, to be seduced by the pull of convention or expediency or outside demands. The undertow of schooling, you quickly figure out, can be as strong and stealthy as any ocean's — maybe even more so.

So, how do you resist?

Connections with Colleagues

The first thing to know is, as much as it may seem otherwise at first, you're not alone. I've spent significant time in dozens of Chicago schools during the past 13 years, and while many have their share of adults who have become, at least on the surface, jaded or resigned to mediocrity, I've also found dedicated, caring, even visionary teachers almost everywhere I've been. This is important to understand as a new teacher because it makes it less likely that you'll fall into the trap of seeing yourself as the anointed one, the lone crusader working for justice in an unjust school and world. Heroic teacher memoirs and Hollywood movies notwithstanding, that is rarely, if ever, the way things are.

While the organizational structures and scheduling at your school may not support alliance-building among teachers (and may, in fact, implicitly encourage you to isolate yourself), one of the best things you can do for yourself as a beginning teacher is seek out allies — both within your school and in the broader community of educators. Fellow teachers with whom you are aligned philosophically and politically can be vital sources of both emotional support and practical ideas, and even those who don't seem to share your views can sometimes prove helpful. A colleague who's been teaching in your building for 25 years, even if "traditional" or "burned out" at first glance, may still have lessons to impart and useful advice to offer, and may, in time, turn out to be not as one-dimensional as you originally thought.

That's not to say that you should expect to be surrounded by hopeful and forward-thinking educators. Cynicism can be deeply entrenched in big-city public schools, and it's also wildly contagious. One of the first temptations for a new teacher is to join this chorus of negativity and begin, however reluctantly, to recite the sorts of excuses you were certain you'd never make: that you can't really get to know your students because there are too many of them, that you can't engage students in group work because they get out of control, that you can't focus on building critical thinking skills when your kids are having a hard enough time just finding a vocabulary word in the dictionary.

I've heard myself say or think all those things at one time or another, and they're all legitimate dilemmas. But Bill Ayers, longtime educator and author of *To Teach,* points out that focusing on all the impediments to your work, while perhaps therapeutic in the short term, is ultimately a dead-end for the committed teacher. Ayers suggests turning each obstacle around and viewing it from a more hopeful perspective by saying, "OK, this is my situation, these are the realities. Given that, what can I do?" Maybe you can't do everything you'd planned or imagined — at least not right away — but you can always do something.

Starting Small

It may be that you have to start with something small and seemingly insignificant — like bulletin boards, for instance. In many schools, bulletin boards simply become part of the scenery, wallpapered with routine announcements or seasonal messages that rarely provoke thought or cause anyone — kids or adults — to stop and take notice.

But bulletin boards can be to teachers and students what blank walls are to graffiti artists: an opportunity — the most visible one of all in many schools — to make a statement, to pose questions, to speak out on an issue, to bring kids' lives into classrooms or hallways. In one school I visited last year, I saw a bulletin board that featured the words "They Were Here First" at its center, with the names of a number of Native-American tribes radiating around the outer edges. At another school, students displayed what they'd learned about the AIDS epidemic in several African countries. Still another teacher put up a thought-provoking quote along with an invitation for students to attach quotes that they found challenging or inspiring.

Those may not sound like such radical acts when placed alongside the more elaborate proposals of education's critical theorists. But once you're in a classroom of your own, you begin to realize that it's in the details, as much as in the big-picture theorizing, that critical conceptions of teaching find life. Kids can learn about equity and justice from the way community is formed in a classroom, how decisions are made, who is represented on the walls and bookshelves, what sorts of interactions are encouraged and discouraged, whose thoughts and ideas are valued, and, yes, even what's on the bulletin boards. Teaching for social justice, in practice, is as much about the environment you create as it is about the explicit lessons you teach.

The Question of Content

Content does matter, though, and it's another area in which, as a new teacher, you'll be challenged to hold true to your beliefs. For one thing, it's likely that you'll feel the ominous cloud of high-stakes testing looming over every curricular decision you make, dictating your answer to the perennial curriculum question: What knowledge and experiences are most worthwhile for my students? Beyond that, you may be further overwhelmed by all you need to do in order to make what you teach more meaningful and critical: limiting the use of biased and oversimplified textbooks, bringing in primary source documents, connecting topics to real-world issues, reading whole novels instead of chopped-up basal selections, giving students opportunities to write about their lives, weaving the arts throughout your subject areas, inviting your kids to help decide what they want to study, and so on.

The scope of the challenge can be truly paralyzing: Because you can't do everything, you delay doing anything, and instead fall back on using textbooks and following directives until you get your feet more firmly on the ground. But the ground is always shifting when you're a teacher, so your feet may never be fully planted. Instead of waiting for that to happen, why not take on something more manageable: Start with one subject and commit yourself to bringing it to life for your students. Or, if you teach only one subject to several groups of kids, try putting your own spin on things one day a week, and try to build from there. Again, you may not be able to do everything you'd hoped all at once — but you can do something.

Balancing Freedom and Control

If you're coming into the classroom with an orientation toward teaching for social justice, you already understand that, although they have helped many people, in many ways public schools have served as an oppressive force in the lives of poor children and students of color throughout this country's history. I had that shameful legacy in mind when I started out as a new teacher, and I wanted to do my part to interrupt it. But my approach, at least initially, was overly simplistic: If schools were oppressive, I figured, then the antidote to that was freedom, so in my classroom students would be "free." It sounded great in my head, but since I hadn't thought out the specifics of what freedom really meant within the context of a public school — or how I might create the conditions where it could happen — I quickly found myself in the midst of absolute chaos in my classes.

Not only does chaos in your classroom make you crazy, but it directs all your energy toward addressing student misbehavior. Other concerns — such as whether your kids are learning anything — lessen in importance. These skewed priorities are often reinforced by administrators who place a premium on order and control, and who hold up as exemplary those teachers who keep the tightest reins on their students. If you're not careful, you may find yourself falling unwittingly into a similar pattern of thinking: classifying your days as good or bad based solely on how quietly your students sit at their desks or how straight a line they form in the hallway.

Many young teachers think they'll be able to rise above such nonsense once they have a classroom of their own, or they delude themselves with the belief that they'll be viewed as such cool teachers that they won't have to worry about disciplinary issues. Progressive approaches to teaching often encourage such an attitude by glossing over classroom management concerns, or by suggesting that if teachers simply come up with engaging lessons, management issues will largely take care of themselves. But my experience is that, in many urban classrooms, it's far more complicated than that, and if you're blindsided by serious discipline concerns, as I was, you can feel compelled to adopt draconian corrective measures.

The point is not to obsess over order and control as a beginning teacher, but to go in with a specific plan of action rather than vague notions about "freedom." If you really want to have an open and democratic environment in your classroom, you have to be thoughtful and purposeful in creating structures that support it.

These details of practice — creating an environment for learning, rethinking your curriculum, and fostering a democratic community — can all provide opportunities for bringing a social justice perspective into your classroom. But it's also possible to become lost in the everyday details, to get so caught up in the immediacy of your teaching that you don't pay enough attention to its larger contexts. Indeed, the undertow may pull you in such a direction: Professional development seminars and inservice workshops frequently encourage tunnel vision in new teachers by focusing narrowly on specific methods, strategies, or one-size-fits-all approaches.

That's why it's important to remind yourself that methods and other practical matters mean little unless placed within a social, political, and economic context. For beginning teachers at urban schools — especially for those who are coming in as "outsiders" to the communities where they're teaching — committing to continued efforts at self-education on issues of race, culture, and poverty is vital (and also something you're not likely to get at an inservice). Middle-class teachers who lack a personal understanding of poverty and the many ways it can impact children, families, and neighborhoods need to do all they can to increase their awareness. Likewise, white teachers need to work hard to learn about the cultural histories and current struggles of their students of color and, at the same time, to examine their own privilege.

Angela Valenzuela, a professor at the University of Texas-Austin, has written that "a community's best interests are served by those who possess an unwavering respect for the cultural integrity" of the people in that community. Clearly, that requires sincere and sustained effort on the part of "outsider" teachers, but it's far from impossible.

Holding On to Hope

No matter what you do to buoy yourself as a new teacher, you're almost certain to have moments — maybe quite a few of them — when you question the value and effectiveness of what you're doing. One of the most persistent early challenges for a socially conscious teacher — at least it was for me — is fighting the feeling that your work isn't making a difference, or at least not the sort of difference you'd imagined. When your goals are expansive and hopeful, when you believe that teaching is potentially a world-changing act, it can become discouraging to feel continually as if your efforts are falling far short of that vision. As one young teacher I know put it, "You feel like you should be seeing light bulbs going off in kids' heads every day, like they're suddenly seeing the world differently. But a lot of times, you think, 'this whole week — nothing! I'm not teaching for social justice!'"

At times like those, the undertow pulls in the direction of fatalism, despair, and emotional disengagement. It beckons you to stop trying so hard, to be more "realistic" about the kids you teach, and to abandon your belief that public schools can be transformed in a meaningful or lasting way. Resisting that suffocating pull — and holding on to hope instead — requires a delicate balancing act: acknowledging the grim systemic realities and personal limitations you face as a teacher, but at the same time re-committing yourself to working toward something better. You have to forgive yourself for your failings, then turn around and try to use them to re-focus and re-energize your teaching the next day.

You also have to allow yourself to appreciate the good moments that do take place in your classroom — no matter how small they may seem in the grand scheme of things. In the words of the poet and novelist Audre Lorde, "Even the smallest victory is never to be taken for granted. Each victory must be applauded, because it is so easy not to battle at all, to just accept and call that acceptance inevitable." I think every new teacher should have that quote taped to her desk, her classroom door, her rearview mirror, her refrigerator, her alarm clock — to any spot where she might need a little extra strength for the journey.

Becoming a teacher is a journey, afterall — one in which you're always learning. One thing I learned while writing this piece is that there's actually no such thing as an undertow. The force of water that pulls you down the beach is called a longshore current, and the one that pulls you out to sea is known as a rip current. Undertow, it turns out, is a colloquialism. Considering that my mother was born on a farm in Georgia and raised in rural Kentucky, it makes perfect sense that that's the term she's always used. Longshore currents and rip currents will probably always be "the undertow" to me.

I learned one more thing, too. If you ever find yourself caught in a real rip current, the best approach is not to try to swim directly against it: You'll exhaust yourself, and the current's force will end up pulling you out anyway. Instead, say those who are knowledgeable in the science of wave motion, you should avoid panicking, swim with the current for a little while, and eventually you'll be free.

The undertow of schools, in my experience, doesn't release teachers from its pull quite so easily. Still, burnout being what it is, there is something to be said for new teachers not trying to fight it at every turn. The best advice, I think, is to choose your battles early on, pace yourself, swim with the current when you have to, and never lose sight of that spot on the shore. ■

Moving Beyond Tired

"We who believe in freedom cannot rest."

— Sweet Honey in the Rock

I was tired. But I had heard that these Rethinking Schools people were hot, really hot. I just had to go and see. I walked up the steps of a typical old-style Portland home. I heard voices coming from inside. Would I be welcome? What was the point? Wouldn't a plate of spicy chili noodles and a bad video be a better way to spend a Friday night? It was my first year of teaching, and I was exhausted.

I knocked and pushed the door open. I placed the token bottle of apple juice on the dining room table, next to three other bottles of juice, a plate of brownies, a bowl of popcorn, and some chips. I kept thinking about those hot chili noodles.

Someone I vaguely knew started speaking to me. I nodded and smiled and pretended I understood everything and was energized and interested. I still wanted to be on my couch, comatose and regenerating from teaching five classes in four different subjects: two classes of law for freshmen, including several who couldn't read; an English class for freshmen, including several who wouldn't read; and two global studies classes that included many students who didn't care.

BY
S.J.
CHILDS

How would coming to this scraggly group of inspired, committed teachers do me any good?

Fighting the Isolation

The meeting was held by the Portland Area Rethinking Schools group (PARS), a network of teachers who meet around issues of equity and education quality. The group holds a "Thank Goodness It's Friday" potluck about every six weeks, and over the years the group's teachers have played an important role in education politics within the district, the city, and throughout the state.

My first PARS meeting focused on the effect of a property-tax cut on education and how we could stop the budget-cutting madness. There was talk of publishing articles, signing petitions, lobbying legislators. There were plans for parent meetings and phone trees. It all sounded great. But I was too tired to do more than listen.

That was several years ago. I would like to say that listening to that energetic and committed group got me out of my isolation and exhaustion. But it didn't. Not because it couldn't, but because I wouldn't let it. Instead, I stayed in my classroom by myself, working day and night to create curricula about social justice.

I didn't go back to another meeting for years. What kept me away is probably what has kept other teachers in the city from coming, has kept other teachers in other states from creating similar groups. It wasn't that their causes weren't my causes or their goals not my goals. It definitely wasn't the people.

But I just couldn't figure out where they got the energy and the time to have all those meetings. My students always came first. I love teaching, and I put all I could into creative and critical lessons. There wasn't much left over for meeting and organizing and fighting back.

The standards and testing movement convinced me I needed to start going to the PARS meetings. I needed to fight back. I realized that if I didn't start participating, everything I loved about teaching might be lost. If I didn't become one of those "hot" people who always have meetings, my classroom could be reduced to a tedious nonsensical world of rote memorization and multiple-choice testing. And the thought of that made me sick to my stomach.

But I have come to realize that it was also more than that. It's also about community, and hope, and inspiration. PARS member Jackie Ellenz described it well: "Meetings are our churches," she said.

PARS members are devoted and dizzy with the possibilities of change. They come back again and again because the meetings are a promise, a way to keep hope alive, a way to help teachers find each other. Through their connections and experiences in PARS, members know they can speak up and not be alone. They have learned how to organize and how to stay strong. They respect and admire one another. Over and over again, members have told me that while it's the political issues that create the need to join, it's the people in the organization that keep them coming back.

The Conclusion of My Tired Story

When I think about it, that is why I am going to those meetings. I go because the meetings give me a sense of connection and community. I can listen to the critical reflection of my peers and know that I am in good company. They make me feel good about teaching when usually there is no one else but my students to cheer me on. My colleagues are no longer people with whom I sit in a lunchroom and groan about the students or the administration. These are people whose thoughts and actions keep me excited.

The meetings help create community — not just because they allow for focused collective conversation, but because they provide the human contact that is so vital to the profession yet might not otherwise happen. Now I am not only going to the meetings, I speak on panels and lead sub-committees.

Today, while my 2-year-old daughter is napping in the next room and I could be reading student papers, I am baking banana bread for this afternoon's TGIF. I think about what Linda Christensen told me, about her daughters who are now 15 and 18.

"My kids have grown up as activists," she said. "I see it in them now. I have given them a model for how to respond when things are unfair."

What greater gift can we give to our students and our children than the inspiration that comes from seeing us struggling for social justice? ■

Unwrapping the Holidays

REFLECTIONS ON A DIFFICULT FIRST YEAR

My teaching career began on the picket line. After I was hired to teach first grade in a small town outside of Seattle, I spent my first month in front of the school instead of in the classroom. After 30 days, our union settled the strike and won smaller class sizes for first and second grade, better health benefits, and a slight raise in salary. And on a personal level, I felt that I had really bonded with my colleagues. Most of the teachers who worked at this school had been born and raised in that small town and they showed extraordinary kindness to me, an outsider, during the strike. My father was having major surgery and I was extremely sad and worried. Each day, teachers inquired about his health. Others showed concern about my lack of income and brought me bags of food. One teacher, Joseph, even brought me several bags of plums from his tree.

But through the course of the year, many of the bonds we formed on the picket line dissolved as I became involved in a controversy over holiday curriculum.

BY DALE WEISS

Before I became a teacher, I had spent years as a political activist. I saw my work as a teacher as important political work and wanted to create a classroom where students would learn to challenge biases and injustice and take action against unfair situations. Since this way of viewing the world seemed normal to me, I naïvely assumed my colleagues — with whom I experienced solidarity on the picket line — shared the same world view. I could not have been more wrong.

Holiday Decorations

Before Thanksgiving, two sixth-grade girls approached me to ask if my first graders could make ornaments for the Christmas tree in the library.

I replied: "We have been learning about four different winter celebrations — Kwanzaa, Hanukkah, Christmas in Mexico, and Winter Solstice, and we are in the process of making a book about each celebration. We could put our books in the library for other children and teachers to read as our contribution." The sixth-grade girls were persistent and still wanted to know if I would have my students make ornaments.

"I don't think so," I said, and then returned to my classroom.

I remember wondering if I would be depriving my students of something by my decision, but in my heart I felt I was doing the right thing. I was teaching them that not everyone celebrates Christmas, that there are many celebratory practices in the month of December, and that each celebration is richly marked with unique customs and beliefs. Not making Christmas ornaments, I decided, would not rob my students of anything — except the belief that only Christmas occurred in December.

Thinking about the Christmas tree in the library and feeling that holiday decorations should reflect diversity, I decided to speak with my principal, Oscar. I told him that I thought public areas in the school should reflect as much diversity as possible. Oscar was very supportive but he cautioned me that many staff members might not agree with my opinions.

At our next staff meeting I expressed my concern about the public Christmas displays and also mentioned the four different December celebrations we were studying in my classroom. And I shared my recent experience with Lindsey, a child in my classroom who was a Jehovah's Witness. Her mother had expressed concern about the class study on Christmas in Mexico. After I explained that our study emphasized the cultural and not religious aspects of the celebration, the parent was relieved. I had told Lindsey's mother that as a Jew, I also did not celebrate Christmas. The next morning Lindsey ran up to me, gave me a big hug, and said, "My mom told me you don't celebrate Christmas either. Now I'm not the only one." I shared this as an example of the pain children can experience when they don't fit in. I also felt responsibility as an educator to minimize that pain in whatever ways I could.

As the meeting ended, two staff members thanked me for opening their eyes to new ways of looking at things. But mostly there was silence. Later in the day I heard, secondhand, that Robert, the librarian, was upset about what I had said during the staff meeting. When I approached him, he said he felt blamed for the library decorations, despite the fact it was the sixth graders who had put up the decorations. I told him that I was not blaming him; I was merely concerned about decorations in common areas in the school.

I went to visit one teacher, Linda, during our lunch hour to ask if I had inadvertently offended her. When I got there she was ripping the "Merry Christmas" banner off her wall and saying to a colleague: "We used to be able to do anything we wanted to at Christmas time, but apparently not any more."

I asked if she was referring to what I said at the staff meeting, and she replied, "Well, yes. Plus, I don't teach about Hanukkah because I just don't know how to pronounce all those words. Besides, I just don't feel comfortable teaching about something I don't know much about." I shared that my viewpoints were not only based in my being Jewish — though this is a part of who I am — but because I believe it's important for children to be exposed to different kinds of people, customs, and belief systems. I also shared that I, too, have a hard time teaching something new and that one way I learn is to read books written for children.

Alexis responded: "We're used to doing the same things every year. When December rolls around, we always take out our December boxes and put on the walls whatever is in those boxes. And we really don't think about it. We prefer it that way." Just then the bell rang and our conversation ended.

As the days went on, I noticed lots of Christmas decorations coming off the walls. The library was almost barren. And, where the library Christmas tree once stood, a book was placed on Hanukkah. Though I had stated my hope that decorations should be more inclusive, not that all Christmas decorations should be removed — and certainly not that a book about Hanukkah take their place — what people heard was something quite different.

The following day, Oscar shared with me that my comments at the staff meeting had really stirred things up, and that people had been speaking with him about the meeting all week. He said he wanted to put the issue on the agenda of the upcoming faculty committee meeting, where I represented the first-grade unit.

The next morning I found an anonymous letter in my school mailbox. It said: "Rights for homosexuals next?" I felt incredibly upset and scared. I showed the letter to Oscar and he assured me he would share the contents of the letter with the faculty committee at our meeting on the following day.

When the meeting began, one teacher said she felt it was important for me to understand that teachers had done things a certain way for many years. The holiday curriculum was not offensive, she contended, because it was well within the district's student learning objectives. I repeated what I had said at the staff meeting and said that it had not been my intent to hurt or offend anyone and if I had, I was truly sorry. Another teacher piped up that she had taught for 20 years — compared to my two-and-a-half months — and she felt no need to explain her curriculum to me. She ended by reminding me "to check things out before jumping to conclusions about the way things are done at our school."

I thought a lot about what she said. I always had seen myself as a person with a commitment to understanding other peoples' views, and as someone who takes the time to talk things through. I have never been comfortable with people coming in from the outside and trying to change things immediately. I wondered if I had become that kind of person. When I first noticed the Christmas tree in the library and had thoughts that holiday decorations should reflect diversity, I had shared this with Oscar prior to saying anything at the staff meeting. Should I have checked things out with other teachers as well?

A few other teachers said they wished I had brought up my concerns in October, before the holiday decorations went up. I replied that as a new teacher, I wanted to wait and see what happened, rather than assuming how things would end up. I thought I was sitting back, waiting and watching — but others saw me as a newcomer barging in, and doing so too late.

Joseph, the same man who had kindly brought me bags plums on the picket line, then said: "You know, several of the staff of Germanic background are extremely upset by the fact that the Christmas tree in the library was removed and a book on Hanukkah was put in its place." I was shocked. It would have been one thing if Joseph had simply said "several staff," but adding "of Germanic heritage" meant something very different. It felt like a brief look into the hatred of the Nazis towards the Jews.

I said that I had no idea who removed the Christmas tree, and that whoever did had done so at their own discretion. I also said I didn't know who put the book on Hanukkah in its place.

Oscar then shared the contents of the anonymous letter I had received, saying it was an example of how far things had gone and how ugly they had gotten. People were shocked and could not believe that "someone from a staff as kind as ours could have done something like this."

As the meeting came to a close, Oscar reiterated the importance of openly speaking with one another when differences occurred, and that talking behind people's backs would only serve to divide the staff further. He said he hoped the staff could heal and move forward with understanding.

Oscar checked on me several times during the day, letting me know how offensive he found Joseph's comment about "staff of Germanic heritage." I appreciated his support and made sure to tell him so.

Misunderstandings

Prior to the faculty committee meeting, I had not realized the extent of misunderstanding and anger that existed. I felt scared and continued to search my mind for who might have put the anonymous letter in my mailbox. Up until the prior week I had looked forward to each day of teaching with great eagerness and pleasure. I now dreaded coming to school.

I felt trapped, wondering if the only way out was to join the opinion of the majority. But finally I realized I couldn't trade my beliefs for a few moments of "relief." Instead, what seemed to pull me through was a feeling of strong empathy for all who struggle for something that is right. I thought about people throughout history who took the first step — and sometimes alone — to raise awareness about an injustice. I thought about people who have risked so much while working to bring about a more just world, who stand on the shoulders of those who came before them and know they must keep trying. It was an empathy that forced me to keep trying as well.

In the days that followed, a few staff members offered their support, for which I was immensely appreciative. I thought back on the first days of picket duty, when relations with my co-workers seemed so promising. I was glad for these memories. They helped soften the present wounds.

At the same time, I had to acknowledge that while the strike served to unify the staff and was a way for me to become acquainted with my colleagues, sharp differences also existed. They were differences that went beyond whether or not someone was nice.

I had popped open a huge can of worms, too big to shut. My original intent was not to change others but to see more diversity reflected in the library and other common areas within the school. But what I had thought was a simple request upset the teaching foundations of many teachers, caused resistance and upheaval, and resulted in my alienation from many staff members.

It was a long year, that first year of teaching. I tried my best to remain cordial with my colleagues, something that was often difficult — yet important — to do. In

VOICES
FROM THE
CLASSROOM

"ALL TEACHING IS POLITICAL whether we're conscious of it or not. We all make political decisions every day in the classroom. If we decide to put up a Halloween bulletin board instead of a bulletin board that indicts Christopher Columbus for being a war criminal, that's a political decision. If we decide to make Valentine's Day hearts with kids instead of celebrating Black History Month, that's a political decision. And it's OK to do some of those things — I'm not against Halloween or hearts, although I oppose a holiday-driven curriculum — but we should do things self-consciously and recognize the political nature of our work."

— Bob Peterson

January of that year, Oscar shared with me he would be leaving for the remainder of the school year due to poor health. He left in February, and his replacement, Jeanne, offered me incredible support — both as a new teacher and as someone attempting to teach from a social justice perspective. This definitely helped me finish out the rest of the school year. (Before the school year ended, Oscar died. It is to his memory and his support of me, and belief in me that first year, that I have always dedicated my life as a teacher.)

I remained at that school one more year, at which point I transferred to a school in Seattle.

Lessons Learned

Introducing change into a school environment — especially one that has been firmly established for many years — is a complex process, one that I vastly underestimated. While I don't condone the reactions of many of my colleagues, I do feel I understand what precipitated their response.

What I have come to think of as "The December Incident" provided several valuable lessons for me.

First, I had not sufficiently assessed the staff's potential reactions to being asked to be more inclusive in the school's December celebrations. I assumed I "knew" the staff because we had walked the picket line for 30 straight days. I naïvely equated solidarity around union issues with pedagogical agreement. Additionally, I was the first new teacher to be hired at this school in many years, and I was viewed as an outsider, a fact I had not adequately appreciated.

Second, I did not take into consideration that many teachers held negative attitudes toward the administration because of the strike that began our school year. Although the strike was over, the administration was still viewed by many as the "enemy." And so my positive rapport with Oscar was viewed by some teachers as me aligning myself with the administration.

Finally, what I am now able to recognize years later is that for the staff of my school, the celebration of Christmas represented much more than merely honoring a holiday that falls in December. It represented an entire belief system and something they valued and wanted to pass on to their students.

If I could turn back time, I would definitely do things differently. I would sit through a "Christmas season" first, modeling my own beliefs within my classroom, but not pushing for change within the entire school. By allowing Christmas to happen first "as it always has," I would better be able to assess people's attachments to doing things in a particular way. I would then bring up the "Christmas issue" in the spring when it might not be so emotionally charged.

I would start by assessing people's viewpoints and beliefs instead of assuming they would understand or desire to do anything differently. For example, my co-workers prided themselves on being nice. They heard my request for diversity as meaning they had not been nice to people who do not celebrate Christmas. While I believe that they misinterpreted my intent, I also think that I was partially responsible for this. I went about things in a way that did not first acknowledge the values held by most of the staff. Perhaps if I had first acknowledged how important the Christmas season was to the vast majority of the staff, they might have been more open to adding a bit of diversity to what to them was the "normal" way of celebrating December. Since I didn't start by acknowledging their values, their defenses were up, and they did not hear what I was trying to say. As a result, people clung more tightly to their own belief systems, and my efforts essentially moved things backwards.

I also did not fully consider that people's reactions to me might be based on the fact I was a first-year teacher. I can now see that not all veteran teachers — particularly those who have shaped the school culture and prefer things to stay a particular way — welcome new teachers with open arms.

I spent most of my first teaching year trying to meld the world of my political activism with the new world I was entering as a teacher. I assumed my passionate devotion to my values could enhance the existing curriculum.

I still believe that our best teaching occurs when we live first as authentic human beings, so I would never advocate leaving one's values at the classroom doorstep. I would, however, suggest a balance of caution and wisdom when embarking on this delicate journey. ∎

Getting Students Off the Track

"Just make it through the year," said the teacher sitting next to me at one of the first English department meetings of the school year. "Wait to think about what worked and what didn't until it's all over."

And though my colleague was trying to be supportive, his words served as a reminder that many teachers — both new and seasoned — think that a new teacher's major goal is to survive the school year.

I was feeling overwhelmed. I had just been hired as an English teacher at Cleveland High School in Portland, Oregon. I was teaching two freshmen honors classes, two sophomore "regular" classes, and one senior honors class. But I didn't want to put my head down and plow through the year, only to look up in June as my students walked away. I wanted to think about what was happening in my classes and in my school.

I decided to approach my year from a place of inquiry — and this grew into an effort to dismantle the tracking system that was in place in our school.

BY
JESSIE
SINGER

I bought an artist's sketch book and used it to jot down thoughts about individual classes, students, department meetings, and my school as a whole. I found time between classes, during meetings, and with students to take note of my teaching life. This journal provided a place for me to record thoughts that I would have otherwise allowed to float away without notice. I used my journal to ask questions: Where can I find poems that speak to these students? Why does Kyle always sit in the back and never take off his backpack? Where is the heart of this school?

Cleveland is a predominantly white (77%) urban school serving 1,300 students in the heart of Southeast Portland. One of the first things I noticed was the way students were divided into two groups: honors and regular. Honors is the name assigned to all classes where students earn honors credit by taking the class, and regular classes are the classes that are considered less challenging and move at a slower pace. The content in these classes is not parallel. Although I had taught for one year in a public high school in Eugene, Oregon, I had never taught in a tracked system and I was naïve about the divisions, assumptions, and learning cultures created and perpetuated through tracking.

I participated in the Portland Area Rethinking Schools Steering Committee, a group of new and experienced teachers, parents, and community members. Our conversations and work together reminded me to trust my voice and instincts. That year, our group's focus was on creating an alternative to the state's system of evaluating schools through standardized testing. We created an Alternative Report Card. I kept thinking about one of the questions from the report card: "Who is represented and honored in the school? Consider hallways, library, and overall school environment." New questions began to form as well: How are students separated by social class, gender, and/or race? How does the language we use as educators mask or perpetuate divisions among students? In what ways does my school provide places for students to feel connected and seen as members of the same community? Are all students given equal opportunities to succeed?

Gathering Data

As I walked to my classroom each morning, I looked at the school with the eyes of an anthropologist gathering data. And I began to notice that my regular students were not given a place in my school. Their faces were not photographed as members of student government, their names were not in the entryway's honor roll, they were not members of the yearbook staff or the newspaper. Many of them worked half time and some even full time at after-school jobs. Many students had responsibilities caring for younger siblings or ailing grandparents.

One issue of the school newspaper printed an article with an enlarged photo of a line-up of Honda Accords and seniors standing in front of each car. The article said the Honda is the most desired and owned car at Cleveland High School. One of my sophomores walked into class that day and said, "Who does this paper think it's talking to? I wish I had a car — don't they get that some of us have to use the city bus?"

I noticed that the daily line-up in front of the discipline vice-principal's office was often made up of regular students and — more often than not — students of color. I noticed how some counselors visited only honors classes to hand out college and scholarship information. I went to the counseling office to ask a counselor about this policy. She said, "Well, this saves me time. I mean, it's clear that the other kids aren't going on to study. If they were, they would be in honors classes."

It became obvious that the choice to be in honors does not happen from year to year — or at all — in high school. My second period senior honors class was made up of 32 students, most of whom had been together since first grade. They often shared stories from fifth grade and then laughed together like a family that had built a collection of shared stories through the passing of time. These students not only shared a history; they also shared a culture. Here they were in high school, in my classroom, together again for one last year of English. School authorities had designated these students as honors students from the day they entered elementary school.

The makeup of my regular classes was more diverse: They came from the poorer and less respected middle and elementary schools. Many students were recent transplants to Oregon. Some had transferred school districts or bused across town, hoping to get away from a rough start somewhere in the past.

As I observed the differences in my classes, I wanted to know more. I talked to my curriculum vice-principal about my concerns, and together we looked up the zip codes of students in honors and regular classes and found that more than 90% of honors students came from the affluent neighborhood that fed into our school.

I carried my curiosity about my students and school into my

teaching practice. I approached student papers, conversations, notes, and absences as data that could inform me more about my teaching and school culture. This approach to my teaching changed my outlook as an educator. The blur of bells, phone calls, attendance notices, overflowing classes, daily plans, piles of papers, meetings, and new curriculum became less overwhelming as I began to see it all from the eyes of a teacher-researcher. When things went well, I asked myself what worked so I could use a successful strategy again. When I came across road bumps in my teaching or with colleagues, I formed questions in my mind or in my teaching journal to collect answers on how to work toward change. My questions made teaching feel like a process instead of a race.

My students became my teachers about what a system of exclusion can do to hinder learning and achievement. Heather, one of my sophomore regular students, started crying when I introduced a unit on college preparation and essay writing. "My counselor told me my freshmen year that I was not college material," she said, "She said I am a regular student and I should just hope to get through the next four years. Why are you making me write a college essay when I am not headed there?"

I was not alone in my inquiry. My neighbor and ally in the east wing was another new English teacher, Deanna Alexich. Her teaching assignment consisted of all regular classes. Deanna's concern was that conversations about curriculum and books did not fit the needs of many of the kids she worked with. At one point she told me, "I feel like

---

VOICES FROM THE CLASSROOM

"WHEREVER YOU ARE, fight for equity and justice, whatever that means at your school. For me, that meant trying to end tracking, opening the canon — and also smaller things like keeping the computer lab open after school. If there's a marginalized group, find a way to create a safe place for them and be their advocate in faculty as well as district- and state-level meetings. Establish safe places for students. Volunteer to advise gay, lesbian, and straight clubs; support student culture groups.

— Linda Christensen

I am tracked in our department because I am not an honors teacher. I'm seen as just a regular teacher and my kids don't matter." Through our discussions, we decided to raise the question of tracking with the English department. As new teachers raising a difficult question, it helped to raise it together.

Deanna and I talked for a few weeks before we decided to bring our thoughts to the department. I was nervous. It is ideas that feel outside the realm of common conversation. Through my conversations with Deanna, we decided that the most effective way to share ideas was through questions. We wanted to invite a dialogue, to hear our colleagues' perspectives, and to see where our conversations led. Now, looking back, I believe that this approach is one of the main reasons that change became possible. It created a safe venue to share ideas.

Who Is Honored?

I started a department meeting asking one of the questions that had been sitting with me for the past weeks: Who is honored here? As soon as this question was asked, the room became uncomfortable. We all knew who was honored at Cleveland, but the question forced us to actually talk about it. This topic was not on my department's agenda, but by asking the question it had to be. I began to share some of my research. As a new teacher, I had an advantage. I felt I had a kind of permission to share my observations as a naïve and new agent.

I began to share the data I had collected throughout the previous months. One of my colleagues, Jim, who is a fellow teacher in the English department, nodded. He said, "As a teacher who has been in this field 25 years, I miss teaching diverse classes with a true mix of kids." As our department began to answer the question of who we honor at our school, we could not avoid the topic of tracking. We all started in different places in the way we talked about our students and teaching. One teacher said, "My regular students are lazy and hard to deal with. I hate having regular classes at the end of the day. They aren't here to learn and they don't care." I added my perspective as a new teacher in the department. "I keep searching for the heart of this school. I can't help feeling uneasy in that the department and system I am a part of are perpetuating divisions among the haves and have-nots." Deanna asked, "What does it say about us as educators if we are only feeling successful with an already successful group of kids? Aren't we failing a huge section of our population?"

That day we all began to ask questions about our teaching and the set-up of our department and school. We began what would become a two-year dialogue and mission to change the way we talk, think, and work with students. This dialogue was not easy. It began from a place of questioning, which led to conversation, and then, more questioning. Our conversations were, and often still are, quite heated. When things get too uncomfortable, we often stop ourselves and restate ideas in the form of questions. This may sound corny, but it works. We have chosen to work toward becoming a department that truly communicates together in order to work toward change. Having true conversations as educators about difficult and important topics means pushing aside smaller differences to focus on a larger vision of equity and justice in our school.

Our department's conversations led us to un-track our ninth grade. We decided that all students should begin their time at Cleveland High School with an opportunity to be seen equally — without pre-assigned labels. As a result of this work, freshmen classes now represent the true population of our school with equal numbers of boys and girls, students from different neighborhoods, and diverse backgrounds. A colleague in my department who was initially resistant to the idea of untracking, walked into my classroom and said, "I love teaching my freshmen classes. In all my years of teaching this age group these classes are more engaged and more fun to teach than any I have taught before." The freshmen team has a common meeting time during fourth period each day to work on ninth-grade curriculum and to discuss teaching strategies, behavioral issues, and successes. This team has presented at districtwide workshops to share our work on untracking. As a result, a neighboring public high school untracked their ninth-grade English classes. At Cleveland, freshmen who struggle significantly with their literacy are offered a second English course called Freshmen Success to work with teachers and tutors on writing development, reading fluency, and homework. A few of the freshmen teachers in the English department are collaborating with teachers in other departments to create Freshmen Academies, where groups of students study multiple subjects together, integrating the curriculum.

As a new teacher, I realized that to see past my own experience meant looking deeply into it. My inquiry process helped to demystify my students, school, and teaching. I learned how to collect data, ask questions, share ideas with a network of support, and instigate change to help create the kind of school I wanted to be a part of over time.

I'm grateful that I did not take my colleague's advice. I didn't wait to think about what worked and what didn't until the end of the year. Inquiry through journal writing, working with other, like-minded teachers, and listening to the concerns of other teachers and students can effect positive change in schools. ■

"We Must Act as if All the Children Are Ours"

AN INTERVIEW WITH PARENT ACTIVIST LOLA GLOVER

The following is condensed from an interview with Lola Glover, director of the parent- and community-based Coalition for Quality Education in Toledo, Ohio. Glover is also a past co-chair of the National Coalition of Education Activists and has served as a co-director of the National Coalition of Advocates for Students. She was interviewed by Barbara Miner.

How did you get involved in education?

I'm the mother of nine children and I started the way most parents do. And that's the PTA, Mothers' Club, room mother, chaperone, chairperson for the bake sales, that kind of thing. This was 30 to 35 years ago.

Because I was at school a lot, I began to notice things that I felt were not conducive to the educational or emotional well-being of students. I began to realize there was a pattern to certain things, instead of something I observed for one day. I began to question those actions, or the lack thereof, and to talk more to my own children about school. It was then that I started to get involved in my children's actual schooling and in academic issues.

I always made sure, however, that I was active in such a way that all the students in that particular classroom or school would benefit, not just my child. When I advocated only for my child, not a lot changed. The teachers and administrators would just make sure that when I was on the scene, or when they dealt with my child, they would do things differently.

I don't believe that we will ever get all of the parents involved in the ways that we would hope. I believe that those of us who have made a commitment to get involved must act as if all the children are our children.

Do you sense that some teachers are reluctant to have parents involved in more than homework or bake sales, that there is a fear that parents are treading on the teachers' turf if they do so?

Absolutely. And I don't think much of that has changed over the years.

Let's say I'm a teacher, and I come in and do whatever I do in my own way, in my own time, and nobody holds me accountable in any way for providing a classroom environment conducive to learning, or for student achievement. I get pretty set in my ways — and defensive with people who might question what I do.

I've found the teachers who are reluctant to have parents involved are those who know they aren't doing the best they can for their students.

Then there are some teachers whose degrees gave them a "new attitude" and who question these folks who didn't graduate from high school, and surely didn't go to college. Such teachers question what these parents are doing in their classrooms. It doesn't matter that they are the parents of their students.

I also have found some really great teachers in our district. They don't have any reservations or problems about parents getting involved in their classrooms or schools. In fact, they welcome and encourage parent involvement.

How can teachers and principals make parents feel more welcome?

One of the biggest mistakes that teachers make is not being in touch with parents until there's a problem. And most parents don't want to hear the problem. They would like to think that little Johnny or Mary is doing fine all the time, and if not, they don't want to hear you putting their kid down. If you start off that way with a parent, it will take some real doing to get on the right foot with them again.

It's not going to be easy to build an alliance with 30 parents, so start with one or two. Get those parents to be your liaisons. Let them know how much you care and what you are trying to accomplish in the classroom. Give them the names and addresses of parents of the kids in your classroom, and ask, "Would you help me contact these parents and explain to them that I would really like to talk to all of them personally." Find out when will be a good time for everyone to meet, and set a date.

Why is it so important to foster mutual respect between parents and teachers?

I am convinced that if students begin to see parents and people in their community and their schools working together, a lot of things would change. First of all, the kids' attitudes would change. Right now, kids' attitudes have not changed about school because they don't see any connection between home and school. They do not see any real efforts being made by either side to come together for the purpose of improving their schools or educational outcomes.

I don't think any of us have

VOICES FROM THE CLASSROOM

"LOCATE THE CULTURES, the history of the community around your school. Who are the local heroes? What groups are working for justice in your school's neighborhood? Who are your allies? Who can your students research? The media puts forward athletes and movie stars as contemporary heroes. Where can they find alternative models in your community?"

— Linda Christensen

the answers to solve these problems. But I do believe that if we come together out of mutual respect and concern, we will make a difference in what happens in our schools and our communities. I know we'll never find the answer if we keep this division between us. For the sake of our children, public education, and our future, we can ill afford not to work together. Make the first move. ∎

So What Is a
Teacher Union Anyway?

Many of us who come to teaching arrive at our first jobs without really knowing what a union is or what purpose it serves. It's not something covered in most teacher education programs. I was lucky. My mother was a telephone operator, so as I grew up there was talk in our house about contracts and negotiations, strikes and picket lines. But many of my colleagues just don't have that experience to draw upon.

So here's a down-and-dirty overview of teacher unions and what they do for us teachers.

The Nuts and Bolts of Union Membership

A union is an organization that advocates for better wages, benefits and working conditions for its members. It's thanks to unions that we enjoy the five-day work week.

There are two national teacher unions: the National Education Association (NEA) and the American Federation of Teachers (AFT). Each has local affiliates in school districts across the country; the NEA also has large state associations. Membership in either of these organizations helps protect you from the arbitrary whims of administrators, false accusations of parents or students, and even

BY
STEPHANIE
WALTERS

unfair layoff or termination from your position.

Depending on where you teach, the protections and benefits offered by your union can vary greatly. In states like Wisconsin, New York, and Ohio, you become a union member by virtue of signing your contract. Once you enter the classroom, you are afforded the protections the collective bargaining agreement (or contract) provides.

There are also states like Florida, Texas, and North Carolina where laws are much less hospitable toward unions and actually prohibit public sector employees (like you) from bargaining for fair wages, hours, and working conditions. These are often referred to as "right to work" states. If you live and work in these locales, unions are much weaker. You have to sign up to become a member of your union, and you are not automatically afforded the rights and protection enjoyed by your counterparts in other states. Sadly, you are often at the mercy of administrators to do the right thing — something that in my experience they do not always do.

To check out what your union has to offer, go to its website: www.aft.org or www.nea.org. Or ask a veteran teacher when the next union meeting is, so that you can attend. You will discover that in addition to representing you, unions provide great benefits that you might never have imagined. (Need some life insurance? NEA can provide it. How about a low-interest credit card? AFT has one for you.)

The most important thing to know now is that teacher unions are built on democratic principles. They're not always perfect, but they usually strive to serve their members as these principles dictate. Members elect presidents, vice-presidents, and building leaders to represent them. Like any democracy, their strength is derived from the active involvement of their members. They need you — the member — to be involved.

Read Your Contract!

I know, I know. As a new teacher you want to make a good impression. You don't want to look like a slacker to your colleagues or your principal. You want to make sure that everyone knows you're willing to go the extra mile for the kids, and take one for the team if need be.

So when the principal comes to you and asks you to volunteer to cover lunch duty one afternoon, you enthusiastically say yes. You want to show her how dedicated you are to the school and that you're willing to help out.

Then she asks you again and again, every day for a whole week. You start to wonder: Is this OK?

Well, the answer is ... it truly depends, and it is very important for you to find out, because you may be getting hosed.

As teachers we usually have rights that are negotiated through our contracts. If you do not have a copy of this very important document, you should obtain one ASAP.

Your contract outlines all the things you're entitled to as an employee of a school district. There is no standard contract: They vary from district to district.

For example, in the Milwaukee Public Schools, teachers are entitled to a duty-free lunch period of 45 minutes. If an administrator is going to assign you to do duty during that period, it can only be for 15 minutes, and you must be paid for that time. There's no way around it: Principals have tried to skirt this rule and they have failed. That's the rule and administrators can't just ignore it. There are consequences if they try.

I know what you're thinking, because at one time I thought it myself: What's a lousy 15 minutes? I'm a professional. I'm dedicated. I don't mind giving a little extra.

Yes, it is true, we are professionals. But if you were an accountant or software engineer, perhaps you'd be able to leave a little early or come in a little later. Not so for teachers. Who would watch the kids? Likewise, taking a longer lunch is definitely out of the question for you. You're a teacher. Can't happen. Your situation is unique.

So there really is a rhyme and a reason for why teachers are in unions, why we have contracts, and why they should be followed.

OK, you're saying, but honestly, you expect me to ask to be paid for a measly 15 minutes?

Well, let's do some arithmetic.

In my school district, a teacher currently earns $21.76 an hour for doing lunch duty. So if you did 15 minutes of lunch duty every day for two weeks, that would total $54.40.

Now multiply that by 20 weeks. That's $1,088.

See what I mean?

Getting a Copy of Your Contract

If you don't have a copy of your district's contract, you should get one, and now! I know that having my contract handy and being able to reference it when I had a question was one of the most important components of my professional development, so much so that I had two copies, one for home and one for school.

In most buildings there is a teacher who volunteers to deal with union issues at the building level. Usually this person is called the building representative or chapter chair. Ask your representative for a copy of your contract. If she doesn't have a copy, she can direct you to your union office, which will be happy to send one out to you. (When I became the representative at my school, I was gladder than ever that I had copies of my contract at home and at work.)

MORE ON TEACHER UNIONS

Teachers first organized themselves into unions in the early and mid-1900s to defend their rights against administrators and school boards. During the past two decades teacher unions have also been instrumental in helping to pass legislation to improve the educational landscape of the country. They have been on the cutting edge of reform of our profession, providing professional development, peer coaching for veterans, and mentoring to new teachers.

This hasn't always been a smooth process, mind you. In 1997 Bob Chase, who was then president of the National Education Association (NEA) angered many union officials when he called for the NEA to "broaden our focus" and "devote as much attention to the quality of the product we produce as we do to our members' wages, benefits, working conditions, and security." Some NEA members worried that Chase was setting up union members to lose hard-won wages and benefits. But Chase remained adamant that teacher unions "cannot afford to continue standing along the sidelines of the education reform debate."

Today many of those tensions remain. But unions have clearly made strides in helping their members become better teachers, while continuing to protect them from unfair treatment on the job.

— Stephanie Walters

Once you get your contract, read it like a letter from home: Study every word. Remember, knowledge is power. The more you know about your rights, the more confident you'll be when you need to take a stand. All the answers might not be in there, but the majority of them will be. If you're unsure about anything you read, ask your representative or contact the union office and speak to a staff person. (Depending on how large or small your district is, there may be only one staff person, and you may have to wait for an answer. Be patient. And be glad you're doing this now, not during a crisis.)

Contracts typically are in effect for two years, then expire. However, everything in the expired contract, including salary, is in force until teachers in your district ratify a new contract. So if you get a copy of your contract from the union and it says it expired last year, relax, it's still good.

Last tip: There will be times that you will encounter an administrator who says, "Do it or else!" Unless it's something that endangers your life or the lives of others, go ahead and do it, then take the matter up with your representative and union officials. ■

For Further Reading

The Rethinking Schools book *Transforming Teacher Unions* presents a vision of "social justice teacher unionism" that challenges teachers and unions to help improve schools and conditions in the broader communities they serve. For more information on this book see page 68.

Authors/Contributors

William Ayers (bayers@uic.edu) is Distinguished Professor of Education at the University of Illinois at Chicago and most recently the author of *Teaching Toward Freedom*.

Bill Bigelow (bbpdx@aol.com) is Classroom Editor of Rethinking Schools and has taught high school for many years in Portland, Oregon. He edited, with Bob Peterson, *Rethinking Globalization: Teaching for Justice in an Unjust World* and *Rethinking Columbus: The Next 500 Years.*

S. J. Childs (sjchilds@spiritone.com) is a teacher, writer, and activist at Franklin High School in Portland, Oregon, and is involved in the Portland Area Rethinking Schools group.

Linda Christensen (lchrist@aol.com) is Language Arts Coordinator for the Portland Public Schools in Portland, Oregon, and a Rethinking Schools editor. She is the author of *Reading, Writing, and Rising Up: Teaching About Social Justice and the Power of the Written Word.*

Rebecca Constantino (rconstan@comcast.net) is a Los Angeles-based education consultant specializing in urban education and literacy development. She is also the founder and director of Access Books, a nonprofit organization that refurbishes neglected school libraries.

Aron Corbett (aroncorbett@yahoo.com) teaches second grade at Hayes Bilingual Elementary School in Milwaukee.

Sara Schneider Cruz (saraschneidercruz@yahoo.com) teaches 5-year-old kindergarten at La Escuela Fratney in Milwaukee.

Lola Glover (MFECQE@aol.com) is Director of the Coalition for Quality Education, a grassroots community organization in Toledo, Ohio, and is a past co-chair of the National Coalition of Education Activists.

Stan Karp (stankarp@aol.com) has taught English and journalism at John F. Kennedy High School in Paterson, New Jersey, for more than 25 years. He is a Rethinking Schools editor and a former co-chair of the National Coalition of Education Activists.

Herbert Kohl (HKHkohl@aol.com) is Director of the Institute for Social Justice and Education at the University of San Francisco. His most recent book is *Stupidity and Tears*.

Enid Lee (enidlee@aol.com) is an internationally known educator, author, and consultant whose work focuses on anti-racism and promoting multiculturalism.

Leon Lynn (rsleon@execpc.com) is the book and website editor with Rethinking Schools in Milwaukee.

Taylor Mali (taylor@taylormali.com), a professional performance poet and voiceover artist based in New York City, spent nine years teaching English, history, and math; he wants to be the person responsible for an entire generation of college graduates considering teaching before business or law school.

Gregory Michie (gmichie38@msn.com) is a Chicago-based teacher and teacher educator. His most recent book is *See You When We Get There: Teaching for Change in Urban Schools*.

Larry Miller (lmillerf@execpc.com) is a Milwaukee Public Schools teacher and a Rethinking Schools editor.

Barbara Miner (rsminer@execpc.com) is a journalist in Milwaukee specializing in education and other social issues. She is a columnist for the journal *Rethinking Schools*, where she previously served as managing editor.

Bob Peterson (repmilw@aol.com) teaches fifth grade at La Escuela Fratney in Milwaukee and is a founding editor of Rethinking Schools. He edited, with Bill Bigelow, *Rethinking Globalization: Teaching for Justice in an Unjust World* and *Rethinking Columbus: The Next 500 Years*.

Kelley Dawson Salas (rskelley@execpc.com) teaches fourth grade at La Escuela Fratney in Milwaukee and is an editor of Rethinking Schools.

Jessie Singer (jsinger14@earthlink.net) taught English at Cleveland High School in Portland, Oregon, and is now a doctoral student in education at the University of California–Santa Barbara.

Kathy Swope (swopekr@mail.milwaukee.k12.wi.us) is Director of the Division of Teaching and Learning for the Milwaukee Public Schools (MPS). She has more than 20 years of experience as an elementary-level classroom teacher, and has served as co-chair of the steering committee of the MPS Multicultural Curriculum Council.

Rita Tenorio (rmmt@aol.com) teaches first grade at La Escuela Fratney in Milwaukee and is a founding editor of Rethinking Schools.

Steve Vande Zande (stevenpolkadot@aol.com) is an artist and an art teacher with the Milwaukee Public Schools, the Milwaukee Art Museum, and Artists Working in Education, and received the 2003 Outstanding Art Educator award from the Wisconsin Art Education Association.

Floralba Vivas (fvivasd@aol.com) was born in Venezuela and teaches fifth grade at La Escuela Fratney in Milwaukee. She is also a pianist and an active chamber musician.

Tracy Wagner (tjwagner@uwalumni.com) teaches ninth-grade English at Charlestown High School, a public school in Boston.

Stephanie Walters (walterss@mtea.weac.org) is a classroom teacher and a staff person for the Milwaukee Teachers' Education Association, the local affiliate of the National Education Association.

Dale Weiss (DMashoya@aol.com) works at La Escuela Fratney in Milwaukee, teaching reading to fourth graders and coordinating a dual-language grant from the U.S. Department of Education.

Index

Notes

Resources from
RETHINKING SCHOOLS

RETHINKING
OUR CLASSROOMS, VOL. 1
Teaching for Equity and Justice

Rethinking Our Classrooms includes creative teaching ideas, compelling narratives, and hands-on examples of ways teachers can promote values of community, justice, and equality — and build academic skills. For teachers K-12.

ISBN 0-942961-18-8 • 216 pp • **$12.95**

RETHINKING
OUR CLASSROOMS, VOL. 2

The new companion volume to the original *Rethinking Our Classrooms* is packed with curriculum ideas, lesson plans, resources, and inspiring articles about teaching. Another invaluable guide to promoting social justice and high-quality student learning.

ISBN 0-942961-27-7 • 240 pp • **$12.95**

RETHINKING GLOBALIZATION
Teaching for Justice
in an Unjust World

A comprehensive collection for teachers and activists including role plays, interviews, poetry, stories, background readings, and hands-on teaching tools. *Rethinking Globalization* is a treasury of information about the threats posed by globalization.

ISBN 0-942961-28-5 • 400 pp • **$18.95**

READING, WRITING, AND RISING UP
Teaching About Social Justice and the Power of the Written Word

Essays, lessons, and a remarkable collection of student writing. *Reading, Writing, and Rising Up* takes us through a language arts curriculum with an unwavering focus on teaching for justice.

ISBN 0-942961-25-0 • 196 pp • **$12.95**

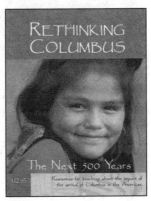

RETHINKING COLUMBUS
The Next 500 Years

Over 80 essays, poems, short stories, interviews, historical vignettes, and lesson plans re-evaluate the legacy of Columbus — right up to the present day. Packed with useful teaching ideas for kindergarten through college.

ISBN 0-942961-20-X • 192 pp • **$12.95**

Rethinking Schools

If you're impressed with *The New Teacher Book*, you'll want to subscribe to our quarterly magazine, *Rethinking Schools*!

Rethinking Schools, the country's leading grassroots education magazine, is written by teachers, parents, and education activists — people who understand the daily realities of reforming our schools. No other publication so successfully combines theory and practice while linking classroom issues to broader policy concerns.

Reasonable Subscription Rates

Three years	$39.95	**(Save over $19 off the cover price!)**
Two years	$29.95	**(Save over $9 off the cover price!)**
One year	$17.95	

Subscriptions to Canada and Mexico add $5 per year.
Other international subscriptions add $10 per year.

FOUR EASY WAYS TO ORDER

1. **Order online:** www.rethinkingschools.org
2. **Call toll-free:** 1-800-669-4192, M-F, 8 am-9 pm (ET)
3. **Fax order to:** 802-864-7626
4. **Mail order to:** Rethinking Schools, PO Box 2222, Williston, VT 05495

"*Rethinking Schools* is an extraordinary publication: the only one I read routinely that reflects the actual experience of teachers, the challenges they face, and the daily work they do."

Jonathan Kozol,
author of *Savage Inequalities* and *Ordinary Resurrections*

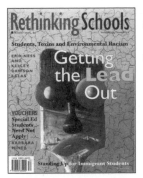

BUSINESS REPLY MAIL

FIRST-CLASS MAIL   PERMIT NO 2222   WILLISTON VT

POSTAGE WILL BE PAID BY ADDRESSEE

RETHINKING SCHOOLS
PO BOX 2222
WILLISTON VT 05495-9940

NO POSTAGE
NECESSARY
IF MAILED
IN THE
UNITED STATES

BUSINESS REPLY MAIL

FIRST-CLASS MAIL   PERMIT NO 2222   WILLISTON VT

POSTAGE WILL BE PAID BY ADDRESSEE

RETHINKING SCHOOLS
PO BOX 2222
WILLISTON VT 05495-9940

NO POSTAGE
NECESSARY
IF MAILED
IN THE
UNITED STATES